PHARMACY LAW SIMPLIFIED

PENNSYLVANIA MPJE® STUDY GUIDE

for 2017 – 2018

By David A Heckman, PharmD

PHARMACY LAW
SIMPLIFIED

Copyright © 2017 by David A Heckman, PharmD

PHARMACY LAW
SIMPLIFIED

DISCLAIMERS & COPYRIGHT

Pharmacy Law Simplified: Pennsylvania MPJE® Study Guide for 2017 – 2018

ISBN-13: 978-1942682073
ISBN-10: 1942682077

MPJE® is a registered trademark of the National Association of Boards of Pharmacy. This publication is neither affiliated with nor endorsed by the National Association of Boards of Pharmacy.

The author does not assume and hereby disclaims any liability to any party for losses, damages, and/or failures resulting from an error or omission, regardless of cause.

This publication is for informational use only.

This publication is not a substitute for legal advice. For legal advice, consult a legal professional.

This publication does not contain actual exam questions.

Copyright © 2017 by David A Heckman
All rights reserved. This book is protected by copyright. No portion of this book can be reproduced in any form, including mechanical or electronic reproduction, without express written permission from the author.

Book cover design by Keeling Design & Media, Inc.

Published by Heckman Media

Printed in the United States of America

TABLE OF CONTENTS

PENNSYLVANIA PHARMACY LAW REVIEW

Pennsylvania Board of Pharmacy	10 – 11
Reports of the Board	11
Pharmacist Licensing	12 – 13
Multiple State Licenses	13
Change of Address	13
Unlawful Acts	14
Refusal to Grant, Revocation, and Suspension of License	15 – 17
Fees, Fines, and Civil Penalties	18
Schedule of Fees	18
Pharmacy Permits	19 – 20
Nonresident Pharmacies	20
Inspection Reports	21
Pharmacy Internships	21
Pharmacist Examination and Licensure	22
Licensure by Reciprocity	22
Pharmacist License and Pharmacy Permit Renewals	23
Continuing Education	24
Noncitizen Eligibility for Pharmacist Licensure	25
Pharmacist Manager	25
Pharmacy Technicians	26
Building Standards	27 – 28
Approval of Plans	29
Sanitary Standards	29
Supplies	30
Equipment	31
Pharmacist Breaks	31
Pharmacy Practice	32
Standards of Practice	33 – 36
Generic Substitution	37
Narrow Therapeutic Index Drugs	38
Prospective Drug Review	39
Patient Profiles	40
Counseling	41 – 42
Central Fill Pharmacies	42
Mailing Prescriptions	43
Controlled Substances	44 – 45
Needles and Syringes	46
Electronic Prescribing	46
Fax Machines	47
Prescription Transfers	47
Emergency Refills	48
Prescription Copies	48
Returning Undelivered Medication to Stock	49
Computerized Recordkeeping	49
Religious, Moral, or Ethical Objections to Filling	50
Collaborative Drug Therapy Management	51
Pharmacist Administration of Injectables	52 – 53
Hospital Pharmacies	54
Drug Therapy Protocols	55 – 56
Long-Term Care Facilities	56
Automated Medication Dispensing Systems	57

Physician Assistant Prescribing 58
Certified Registered Nurse Practitioner Prescribing 59
Certified Nurse Mid-Wife Prescribing 59
Optometrist Prescribing 60
Poisons .... 60 – 61
Radiopharmaceuticals 62
Advertising 62
Naloxone 62
Controlled Substances – Select Examples .... 63 – 67

FEDERAL PHARMACY LAW HIGHLIGHTS
The Roles of Government Agencies 69
Federal Controlled Substances Act .... 70 – 74
Drug Addiction Treatment Act of 2000 75
Methadone Dispensing Restrictions 75
DEA Forms 76
Professionals with Prescribing Authority 77
DEA Number Verification .... 78 – 79
Institutional DEA Numbers 80
Combat Methamphetamine Epidemic Act of 2005 81
Poison Prevention Packaging Act of 1970 82
Omnibus Budget Reconciliation Act of 1990 82
Health Insurance Portability & Accountability Act 83
Generic Substitution and the Orange Book 84
Federal Food, Drug & Cosmetic Act 85
Adulterated vs Misbranded 85
Compounding vs Manufacturing 86
Medicaid Tamper-Resistant Prescription Requirement 87
FDA Recalls 88
NDC Numbers 88
Over-the-Counter Drug Labels 89
Restricted Drug Programs .... 90 – 91
Long-Term Care Facility Pharmacy Services 92
Additional Recommended Study Sources 92

INTRODUCTION

PREPARE THOROUGHLY
The MPJE® is notoriously difficult. How can you prepare for this? The answer is **thorough preparation**. There are no secrets. The more familiar you are with state and federal pharmacy laws, the less likely you are to panic when faced with a challenging question.

DEFEAT DISTRACTION
As you prepare for this exam, your biggest enemy is **distraction**. Develop a strategy to avoid distractions now. I recommend studying in a library and leaving your electronic devices at home.

DO NOT TAKE SHORTCUTS
Use this study guide to review key points in preparation for the Pennsylvania MPJE®. Do not use this book as a substitute for a thorough review of the official Pennsylvania pharmacy laws, rules and regulations. Once licensed, you are expected to possess a certain level of professional competence, including knowledge of the pharmacy laws, rules and regulations relevant to your state. To succeed on the exam, and in your professional life thereafter, it is imperative to review the most current version of the Pennsylvania pharmacy laws, rules and regulations as part of your study plan. See page 92 for a list of relevant laws, rules and regulations.

THE INFORMATION IN THIS STUDY GUIDE IS NOT LEGAL ADVICE
This publication was created as an informational exam preparation resource for the Pennsylvania MPJE®. The author is not a lawyer, and the information in this study guide is not legal advice. For legal advice, consult a legal professional.

PROCEED ➲

PENNSYLVANIA PHARMACY LAW REVIEW

PENNSYLVANIA BOARD OF PHARMACY

Who are the members of the Pennsylvania Board of Pharmacy?
- ✓ The Commissioner of Professional and Occupational Affairs.
- ✓ The Director of the Bureau of Consumer Protection in the Office of the Attorney General (or a designee).
- ✓ Two (2) people representing the public.
- ✓ Five (5) people licensed to practice pharmacy in Pennsylvania (cannot be teachers).
  - ⇨ Two (2) pharmacists from independent retail pharmacies.
  - ⇨ Two (2) pharmacists from chain retail pharmacies.
  - ⇨ One (1) pharmacist from an acute care institutional pharmacy.

Who is responsible for appointing members of the Board?
The Governor, with the advice and consent of a majority of the elected Senate.

How much experience must a pharmacist have to be eligible for appointment to the Board?
Five (5) years of experience as a registered pharmacist immediately preceding their appointment.

How long are board member terms?
Six (6) years.

Can a term ever exceed six (6) years?
Yes. A member may serve for up to six (6) additional months while a successor is being appointed and qualified.

How many consecutive terms can one (1) board member serve?
Two (2) terms.

What is a quorum?
The minimum number of members needed to conduct official business.

How many board members must be present to constitute a quorum?
A majority.

Must board members be physically present to count as part of a quorum or to vote on an issue?
Yes.

Who selects the Chairman of the Board?
Each year, the members of the Board select a chairman from among themselves.

Can a member of the Board lose their seat on the Board?
By failing to appear for three (3) consecutive meetings, unless due to illness or a death in the family.

How can a *public member* of the Board lose their seat?
By missing two (2) consecutive mandated training seminars, unless due to illness or a death in the family.

What compensation is a member of the Board entitled to receive?
$60 per day when attending work of the Board plus reasonable traveling, hotel, and other necessary expenses incurred when performing work of the Board.

How frequently is the Board required to hold a meeting?
Once every two (2) months (*minimum*).

The Board has the authority to…
- ✓ Regulate pharmacy practice.
- ✓ Determine the nature of board exams (i.e. NAPLEX® and MPJE®).
- ✓ Examine, inspect, and investigate applicants and applications.
- ✓ Employ inspectors and consultants.
- ✓ Investigate and prosecute violations of the state pharmacy act.
- ✓ Inspect pharmacies.
- ✓ Conduct hearings to revoke/suspend licenses, permits, and registrations.
- ✓ Subpoena witnesses for hearings.
- ✓ Assist other agencies with enforcing pharmacy laws.
- ✓ Promulgate rules/regulations to regulate distribution of drugs/devices.

What is a chain retail pharmacy?
A business operating five (5) or more pharmacies in the state of Pennsylvania.

REPORTS OF THE BOARD

The Board submits an annual estimate of expenses to _____ and _____.
- ✓ The Department of State.
- ✓ The House and Senate Appropriations Committee.

A report of complaints, time to resolve complaints, the status of cases, and board actions taken is made annually to _____ and _____.
- ✓ The Professional Licensure Committee of the House of Representatives.
- ✓ The Consumer Protection and Professional Licensure Committee of the Senate.

PHARMACIST LICENSING

Must you be a citizen of the United States to obtain a pharmacist license in Pennsylvania?
Yes.

What is the minimum age requirement for licensure?
Twenty-one (21) years old.

Can the Board deny an application for a pharmacist license if they believe the applicant has poor moral and professional character?
Yes.

Can the Board deny an application if they believe the applicant is unfit to practice pharmacy due to controlled substance or alcohol use?
Yes.

Can the Board deny an application if they believe the applicant is unfit to practice pharmacy because of mental or physical disability?
Yes.

What is the minimum educational requirement for obtaining a license?
Bachelor of Science in Pharmacy *or* PharmD from an ACPE-approved college or school of pharmacy.

TRUE OR FALSE
The Board may deny an application if the applicant has committed a felony involving controlled substances.
True. The Board may disregard felonies committed more than 10 years prior to the date of application.

SUMMARY OF PENNSYLVANIA PHARMACIST LICENSURE PREREQUISITES

- ✓ US citizen.
- ✓ Age 21 or older.
- ✓ Good moral and professional character.
- ✓ Fit to practice (e.g. no controlled substances or alcohol abuse, no mental or physical disability).
- ✓ Possession of a BS in Pharmacy or PharmD from an ACPE-accredited school.
- ✓ Completion of the required internship experience.
- ✓ Successful completion of the Board exams (NAPLEX® and MPJE®).
- ✓ No felonious acts in violation of the Controlled Substance Act.

Not everyone passes the Board exams on their first attempt. How many times can you take the pharmacist licensing exams?
You can take each exam up to three (3) times in two (2) years.

What happens if you fail a licensing exam three (3) times?
You must complete additional preparation assigned by the Board to qualify for another attempt.

What are the two (2) prerequisites for registration as a pharmacy intern?
- ✓ Completed two (2) years of college coursework.
- ✓ Accepted to or enrolled in an ACPE-accredited school or college of pharmacy.

For what amount of time is a pharmacy intern registration valid?
Six (6) years from the date issued (excluding time spent in the military).

How often must a Pennsylvania pharmacist license be renewed?
Biennially (every two (2) years).

Can you become licensed as an Assistant Pharmacist?
No. Assistant pharmacist licenses are no longer granted by the Board.

Must your pharmacist license be placed on display?
Yes. Your license must be displayed conspicuously in the pharmacy where you work.

MULTIPLE STATE LICENSES

If you possess a pharmacist license in more than one (1) state, territory, or country, must you report the information about the other licenses to the Pennsylvania Board of Pharmacy?
Yes. You must report information regarding all other licenses on the biennial registration application.

If you are disciplined by the board of pharmacy in *another* state, territory, or country, must you inform the Pennsylvania Board of Pharmacy?
Yes. You must report this information on the biennial registration application *or* within ninety (90) days of the final ruling (*whichever is sooner*).

CHANGE OF ADDRESS

TRUE OR FALSE
As a licensed pharmacist, you are required to file a current mailing address with the Board.
True.

When must you notify the Board of any changes in your mailing address?
Within ten (10) days of the change.

When changing the mailing address of a pharmacy, when must the Board receive notification of the change?
Within ten (10) days of the change.

UNLAWFUL ACTS

An agent of the Board shows up at your pharmacy to perform an inspection, but you refuse to let him in. Do you have the right to refuse the inspection?
No. Assuming it is a lawful inspection, you do not have the legal right to refuse an inspection.

Your small-town pharmacy has been put out of business by a large chain competitor. You decide to auction off your entire inventory, including the drugs. Is it legal to auction off your drug inventory?
Yes, *if* the auction has been approved by the Board beforehand.

Note: The Board would appoint a licensed pharmacist to supervise the auction.

In Pennsylvania, certain words *cannot* be used in any manner of advertisement unless the business using those words is registered with the Board as a pharmacy. Those privileged words include...

- Drug store.
- Pharmacy.
- Apothecary.
- Drugs.
- Medicine store.
- Medicines.
- Drug shop.
- Apothecary.
- Pharmaceutical.
- Homeopathy.
- Homeopathic.

Certain titles are also reserved for individuals registered with the Board as a licensed pharmacist. Those privileged titles include...

- Pharmacist.
- Assistant Pharmacist.
- Druggist.

Is it *legal* to buy and/or sell drug samples?
No.

When practicing pharmacy, the following acts are unlawful:

- Deceit.
- Fraud.
- Misrepresentation.
- Subterfuge.
- Forgery.
- Use of false statements.
- Concealment of material fact.

In committing any of the above "unlawful acts," what type of conviction would you be likely to receive?
Misdemeanor.

What is the maximum penalty for committing a misdemeanor?
One (1) year imprisonment and $5,000 fine.

What is the maximum penalty for subsequent offenses?
Three (3) years imprisonment and $15,000 fine.

If your license has been suspended, can you still offer to practice pharmacy?
No. You can only offer to practice pharmacy if you possess a valid, unexpired, unrevoked, and unsuspended license.

The Board collects fees for a variety of activities, including the licensing of pharmacists. Who is responsible for setting the fees?
The Board.

REFUSAL TO GRANT, REVOCATION, AND SUSPENSION OF LICENSE

The Board refuses to issue your pharmacist license. How do you challenge their decision?
You must request a hearing in writing within fifteen (15) days of being notified of the Board's decision.

Hearings are conducted in accordance with _____.
Administrative Agency Law.

Who establishes and publishes procedural rules concerning the conduct of hearings?
The Board.

Are all board members required to be present at all hearings?
No. A majority of the Board designates one (1) or more members to attend a hearing. Subsequently, notes of the testimony are given to each member of the Board.

Why are notes of the testimony provided to each member of the Board?
Because each member must cast a vote on the final decision, regardless of whether they attended the hearing.

How does the Board reach a decision?
All decisions are reached by a majority vote of the entire Board.

You are legally committed to a mental institution. Does this affect your ability to practice pharmacy?
Yes. Your license would be automatically suspended.

You have been accused of committing a felony under the Controlled Substance, Drug, Device, and Cosmetic Act. Does this affect your license?
No. Only a conviction (a judgment of guilt, an admission of guilt, or a plea of nolo contendere (no contest)) will affect your license. If you were convicted, then your license would be automatically suspended.

We know the Board can act against your license if you are physically or mentally disabled/impaired, but how does the Board determine *who* is mentally or physically disabled/impaired?
The Board appoints and compensates a professional consultant who is a licensee of the Board with education and experience in the identification, treatment, and rehabilitation of mental or physical impairments.

Your license was suspended due to mental impairment. How do you get your license back to active status?
1. Form an agreement with the Board to enroll in an approved treatment program.
2. Comply with the terms of the agreement.
3. Make satisfactory progress.
4. Adhere to any limitations on practice imposed by the Board.

If you report that a colleague diverted controlled substances, can you be subjected to civil or criminal charges?
No, not if the report was made in *good faith* and *without malice*.

In the above scenario, what might happen if you neglect to report the controlled substance diversion?
$1,000 fine (*maximum*).

If your license is revoked, how long must you wait before you will be eligible to apply for reinstatement?
Five (5) years (*minimum*).

Note: The same applies to permits and registrations.

Your pharmacist license is framed and hangs on the wall, but it was recently suspended. Do you get to keep your license?
No. After a license has been suspended or revoked, it must be returned to the Board.

What if you do not return the license to the Board?
You would be charged with committing a misdemeanor of the third degree.

If you obtain, or attempt to obtain, a pharmacist license or pharmacy permit by any of the following methods, then the Board will refuse, revoke, or suspend your license.
- Fraud.
- Deceit.
- Misrepresentation.

TRUE OR FALSE
Only felony charges that involve *pharmacy practice* can have a negative impact on your pharmacist license.
False. Although felony charges involving pharmacy practice *can* negatively affect your license, other felony charges, particularly those involving moral turpitude, can also have a negative impact on your license.

How can felony charges impact your pharmacist license?
The charges may cause the Board to revoke, suspend or refuse to grant your license.

When can felony charges have a negative impact on your pharmacist license?
When you are found guilty, plead guilty, plead nolo contendere (no contest), or receive probation without verdict.

What if the felony was committed in another jurisdiction?
This makes no difference to the Board. Felony charges in any jurisdiction can have a negative impact on your license.

What are some personal activities that could cause the Board to refuse, revoke, or suspend your pharmacist license?
- Abuse of alcoholic beverages.
- Abuse of controlled substances.
- Abuse of any other substance that impairs intellect and judgment to the extent it affects performance of professional duties.

Does the Board have authority to make a pharmacist submit to a mental or physical exam?
Yes.

Why does the Board have this authority?
Because a mental or physical disability could render a pharmacist unfit to practice pharmacy.

If you are deemed unfit to practice due to a disability, will you ever be able to practice pharmacy again?
Yes, *if* you can demonstrate your ability to resume competent practice with reasonable skill and safety.

You have a pharmacist license in Illinois that is revoked. Can this lead to revocation of your Pennsylvania?
Yes.

What are other actions could cause the Board to the refuse, revoke, or suspend your license?
- Violating the Pennsylvania Pharmacy Act.
- Knowingly permitting the violation of the Pennsylvania Pharmacy Act.
- Knowingly allowing an unlicensed individual to practice pharmacy.
- Knowingly compounding, dispensing, or selling a misbranded product.
- Committing gross professional misconduct.

What are some examples of gross professional misconduct?
- Willfully deceiving the Board during an investigation.
- Advertising prices for drugs/services without conforming to federal regulations.
- Publically asserting professional superiority.
- Engaging in false, misleading, or deceptive advertising of drugs or medical devices.
- Participating in a rebate (i.e. kickback) agreement with prescribers.
- Misbranding or adulterating any drug or device.
- Buying or selling drug samples.
- Not having your pocket registration card available for inspection when working.
- Accepting returns and then reselling drugs that have left the pharmacy.

Based on the above information, can you make tell customers that you are the best pharmacist in town?
No. This is gross professional misconduct.

A physician owns a pharmacy in the same building where he practices medicine. He hires you as the pharmacist and wants you to dispense prescriptions written by him. He exercises supervision and control over you. Is this arrangement legal?
No. This is also gross professional misconduct. In this type of scenario, you can only be employed by the physician to manage drug therapy. You cannot engage in retail dispensing.

You form an agreement with a local prescriber. As part of the agreement, the prescriber directs a certain number of his patients to your pharmacy. Is this agreement legal?
No. This agreement impinges upon a patient's freedom to select his/her own pharmacy.

If your license is refused, revoked, or suspended due to a violation of the Controlled Substance, Drug, Device, and Cosmetic Act, how long until your license is eligible for reinstatement?
Ten (10) years.

Besides refusing, revoking, or suspending your license, what other actions may the Board take against you?
- Administer a public reprimand.
- Place limitations or restrictions on your license.
- Require care, counseling, or treatment by a physician or psychologist.
- Place you on probation.
- Reissue a suspended license and impose disciplinary or corrective measures.

FEES, FINES, AND CIVIL PENALTIES

How does the Board obtain money to pay expenses?
By collecting fees, fines, and civil penalties.

When can the Board increase fees?
If the Board's expenses exceed the revenue raised (from fees, fines, and civil penalties) over a two (2) year period, then fees can be raised to make projected revenues meet or exceed expenses.

How else can Board fees can be increased?
If the Bureau of Professional and Occupational Affairs determines that fees are too low to support the minimum enforcement efforts required by the state pharmacy practice act, then fees can be raised in consultation with the Board.

When the Board collects fees, fines, and civil penalties, where does the money go?
Into the Professional Licensure Augmentation Account.

SCHEDULE OF FEES

Application for Pharmacy Intern Certificate	$35
Certification of Exam Scores or Intern Hours	$25
Application for Pharmacist License	$45
Pharmacist License Biennial Renewal	$190
Pharmacist License Late Renewal Penalty	$25
License Verification	$15
Application for Approval to Administer Injectables	$30
Approval to Administer Injectables Biennial Renewal	$30
Pharmacy Permit Application	$125
Inspection of New Pharmacy (after failing the first inspection)	$115
Change in Pharmacy Owner or Board of Directors	$30
Pharmacy Permit Change (without inspection)	$45
Pharmacy Permit Change (with inspection)	$125
Pharmacy Permit Biennial Renewal	$125
Pharmacy Permit Late Renewal Penalty	$25
Permit Verification	$15

PHARMACY PERMITS

What Board-required tools must a pharmacy possess to qualify for a Permit to Conduct a Pharmacy?
- ✓ Reference books.
- ✓ Current supplements to reference books.
- ✓ Professional, technical, and pharmaceutical equipment.

Note: The specific tools are determined by the Board based on the type of pharmacy practice you plan to run (e.g. community pharmacy, home infusion pharmacy, compounding pharmacy).

Who is required to oversee a pharmacy at all times?
A pharmacist duly licensed in Pennsylvania.

Note: "Duly" means properly.

Can personal character affect your ability to obtain a pharmacy permit?
Yes. To obtain a pharmacy permit, you must have good moral and professional character.

Is a pharmacy permit required to be on display?
Yes. A permit must be displayed conspicuously in the pharmacy for which it was issued.

Can you operate or advertise a pharmacy prior to obtaining a pharmacy permit from the Board?
No.

What two (2) names must be listed on a pharmacy permit?
- ✓ The pharmacy owner's name.
- ✓ The pharmacist manager's name.

When registering for a pharmacy permit, Frank named his pharmacy "Frank's Family Pharmacy," but a few months later he decided to order a new sign that reads "Frank's Friendly Neighborhood Pharmacy." What does Frank need to do before displaying his new sign?
He will need to get a new permit since a pharmacy cannot display any name other than the name registered with the Board.

When must you obtain a new pharmacy permit?
When there is a change in the name of the pharmacy, the ownership of the pharmacy, or the controlling interest of the pharmacy.

If there is a change in the name, ownership, or controlling interest of a pharmacy, when must an application for a new permit be filed?
Within thirty (30) days of the change.

What must you do when permanently closing or otherwise ceasing operation of a pharmacy?
- ✓ Return the current pharmacy permit to the Board.
- ✓ Inform the Board of where you are sending the prescription files and drugs.

What can be done with the prescription records and drugs after a pharmacy is closed?
The prescription records and drugs can be sold, transferred, or destroyed.

When closing a pharmacy, the pharmacy permit must be returned to the Board in what time frame?
Immediately.

When closing a pharmacy, the Board must be informed of where you are sending the prescription files and drugs in what time frame?
Immediately.

What other action must be taken immediately when closing a pharmacy?
Signs, symbols, and any other indications of a pharmacy must be removed from the interior and exterior of the building.

After closing a pharmacy, are you required to obtain permission from the Board prior to selling, transferring, or disposing of prescription records or prescription drugs?
Only if thirty (30) days have lapsed since the date of closing.

If someone owns one (1) pharmacy and wants to open a second pharmacy, must he/she apply for a second pharmacy permit?
Yes. There must be a separate permit for each pharmacy.

In an institutional setting, are satellite pharmacies required to possess a separate pharmacy permit?
No.

How many pharmacies can a pharmacist supervise at once?
One (1) pharmacy.

NONRESIDENT PHARMACIES

What is a nonresident pharmacy?
In the context of the Pennsylvania Pharmacy Act, a nonresident pharmacy is a pharmacy located outside of Pennsylvania that ships, mails, or delivers Rx drugs or devices into Pennsylvania pursuant to a prescription.

If a pharmacy is permitted to operate in one (1) or more states other than Pennsylvania, then the information regarding the other permit(s) must be reported to the Pennsylvania Board of Pharmacy on the _____.
Biennial registration application.

If another state board of pharmacy takes disciplinary action against a Pennsylvania-registered nonresident pharmacy, then said pharmacy must notify the PA State Board of Pharmacy with _____ of final disposition.
Thirty (30) days.

It is illegal for an out-of-state pharmacy to _____ in Pennsylvania prior to registering with the PA State Board of Pharmacy.
Advertise.

The PA State Board of Pharmacy has the power to _____ the permit of a nonresident pharmacy if the pharmacy's permit is revoked or suspended in another state.
Refuse, revoke, or suspend.

INSPECTION REPORTS

How long must anyone registered with the Board maintain copies of inspection reports or notices?
For two (2) years from the date issued.

How must these records be maintained?
In a readily retrievable manner within the pharmacy.

PHARMACY INTERNSHIPS

What is the purpose of a pharmacy internship program?
To help interns gain the knowledge and practical experience needed to practice pharmacy competently.

What eligibility criteria must you meet to register as a pharmacy intern?
Completed at least 2 years of college *and* accepted or enrolled in an ACPE-accredited pharmacy degree program.

What is the fee for a pharmacy intern certificate?
$35.

When does a pharmacy intern certificate expire?
Six (6) years from the date issued (*excluding any time spent in the military*).

How many experience hours must be completed by an intern as a prerequisite for pharmacist licensure?
1,500 hours.
- ✓ Up to 1,000 hours of which may be obtained through pharmacy school rotations.
- ✓ At least 500 hours of which must be earned independently by working in a pharmacy.

> **Note:** An intern can log no more than 50 hours per week.

When logging independently-earned internship hours, the supervising pharmacist must be registered as a _____.
Preceptor.

TRUE OR FALSE
A pharmacist that is employed part-time cannot register as a preceptor.
True. Only a full-time pharmacist can register as a preceptor.

TRUE OR FALSE
The Board counts all hours spent working in a pharmacy as intern hours, regardless of the nature of the work.
False. The Board only grants credit for hours spent on activities related to the practice of pharmacy.

Can you obtain credit for internship hours earned out-of-state?
Yes, *if* you can satisfy the Board with evidence that the experience was equivalent to an in-state internship.

PHARMACIST EXAMINATION AND LICENSURE

What steps must be completed to obtain a license to practice pharmacy?
- Submit the appropriate paperwork to the Board.
  - ⇨ An application for licensure to the Board.
  - ⇨ Proof of graduation from ACPE-accredited school.
  - ⇨ Affidavits of all internship experience.
  - ⇨ Application fee.
- Register, pay for, and pass the Board exams.
  - ⇨ North American Pharmacist Licensure Exam (NAPLEX®).
  - ⇨ Multistate Pharmacy Jurisprudence Exam (MPJE®).

What is the rate-limiting step in receiving the Authorization to Test (ATT) from the Board?
Filing the internship experience affidavits with the Board.

If caught cheating on a Board exam, how long must someone wait before they can file a new application for examination?
One (1) year.

Who determines when and where the Board exams will be administered?
The Board in conjunction with the test administrator.

Who develops and administers the NAPLEX® and MPJE®?
The National Association of Board of Pharmacy® (NABP®).

What is the minimum passing score for each of the Board exams?
A scaled score of 75.

LICENSURE BY RECIPROCITY

If you are already licensed as a pharmacist in another state, then how do you obtain a Pennsylvania license?
- Apply for licensure by reciprocity through the NABP® website.
- Follow NABP® instructions and send application to Pennsylvania Board of Pharmacy along with a $45 check or money order.
- If licensed after January 26, 1983, then prove that you passed the Federal Drug Law Exam (FDLE).
  - ⇨ If you cannot prove you passed the FDLE, you must pass the Pennsylvania MPJE®.
  - ⇨ If you were licensed before January 26, 1983, then you are not required to take the Pennsylvania MPJE®.

PHARMACIST LICENSE AND PHARMACY PERMIT RENEWALS

When must a pharmacy permit be renewed?
Every two (2) years on August 31st of odd-number years (e.g. August 31, 2017).

What is the fee for renewing a pharmacy permit?
$125.

What is the penalty for renewing a pharmacy permit late?
$25.

When must a pharmacist renew his/her pharmacist license?
Every two (2) years on September 30th of even-number years (e.g. September 30, 2018)

What is the fee for renewing a pharmacist license?
$190.

What is the penalty for renewing a pharmacist license late?
$25.

What documentation must be submitted with an application for pharmacist license renewal?
Proof of compliance with the continuing education (CE) requirement.

TRUE OR FALSE
If you fail to renew a license or permit on-time, you must stop working until the renewal is processed.
True.

In addition to a late renewal penalty, what other charges are incurred when renewing late?
$5 for each month (or fraction of a month) beyond the original renewal date.

What is the procedure for allowing a license to lapse?
- ✓ Using the renewal form, notify the Board that you wish to let your license lapse, and provide a brief explanation of your reasons.
- ✓ With the renewal form, surrender your pocket license and your display license to the Board.

How do you reactivate a license that has been lapsed for one (1) or more years?
- ✓ Show evidence of full-time pharmacy practice in another state during the period of lapsed licensure.
- ✓ If you did not practice pharmacy in another state during the period of lapsed licensure, then complete CE equivalent to the amount you would have been required to complete had you kept the license active.

An institution is not eligible for a pharmacy permit unless the pharmacy is open at least ___ hours per week under the supervision of a pharmacist manager.
Twenty (20).

CONTINUING EDUCATION

How many hours of CE must a pharmacist complete each renewal period (every two (2) years)?
Thirty (30) hours of continuing education.

What portion of the 30-hour CE requirement must be on *patient safety*?
Two (2) hours (effective October 2012).

What portion of the 30-hour CE requirement must be on *child abuse recognition and reporting requirements*?
Two (2) hours (effective January 2015 per Act 31).

> **Note:** Applicants for initial licensure must complete three (3) hours of Department of Human Services (DHS)-approved training on child abuse recognition and reporting requirements.

For pharmacists authorized to administer injectables, how much of the 30-hour CE requirement must concern the administration of injectables?
Two (2) hours.

The Board only accepts CE hours earned through _____-accredited programs.
Accreditation Council for Pharmacy Education (ACPE).

Are non-ACPE-accredited programs ever deemed acceptable by the Board?
Yes. Programs that are not ACPE-accredited can apply to the Board for approval.

> **Note:** Requests for approval must be submitted to the Board sixty (60) days prior to the start of the program.

How does the Board know whether people are actually completing the required CE?
The Board randomly audits 5% of license renewal applicants to determine compliance.

If audited, what documentation would the Board require you to produce?
The certificates granted upon completion of the CE programs.

Does the Board ever audit more than 5% of license renewal applicants?
Yes. If the initial audit reveals a noncompliance rate greater than 20%, then the Board may expand the audit.

What happens if the Board finds that you are noncompliant with the CE requirement?
You will receive a notice of deficiency from the Board, at which point you will have six (6) months to make up the delinquent CE.

If you earn more than thirty (30) hours of CE in a two (2)-year period, can you apply the excess CE to the next renewal period?
No. Excess CE hours cannot be carried over to the next renewal period.

Does the Board require CE to be earned through live programs?
No. The Board accepts live CE and correspondence CE.

For the first license renewal period, are new graduates *exempt* from the thirty (30)-hour CE requirement?
Yes.

If you reciprocate to Pennsylvania in May 2016, must you complete the thirty (30)-hour CE requirement to renew your license in September 2016?
No. For reciprocated licenses, the CE requirement is divided into quarters and the licensee must complete the CE beginning the first quarter following licensure. So, in this case, you would only need 3.75 CE hours (to fulfill the requirement for the 3-month quarter from July – September) to renew your license in September 2016.

NON-CITIZEN ELIGIBILITY FOR PHARMACIST LICENSURE

What is the minimum age requirement for non-citizens to obtain a license to practice pharmacy?
21 years old (same as for United States citizens).

What is the educational requirement for non-citizens to obtain a license to practice pharmacy?
Graduated from a college of pharmacy accredited by the ACPE or another college of pharmacy approved by the Board.

TRUE OR FALSE
If you graduate from a foreign school and obtain a pharmacist license in Pennsylvania, you may not be able to reciprocate your Pennsylvania license to other states.
True.

What conditions must be met for the Board to consider approving a special internship program of less than 1,500 hours (but not less than 500 hours) for the graduate of a foreign college?
- ✓ Has had experience practicing pharmacy.
- ✓ Demonstrates knowledge of American pharmacy practice.
- ✓ Communicates proficiently using the English language.

PHARMACIST MANAGER

When a pharmacist manager leaves his/her position, when must the permit holder inform the Board?
Within fifteen (15) days of the pharmacist manager leaving. Also, the name of a new pharmacist manager must be provided to the Board at that time.

How does the Board indicate approval of the new pharmacist manager?
If the Board does not object within thirty (30) days of notification, then the new pharmacist manager is approved by default.

What if the permit holder cannot find a replacement pharmacist manager within fifteen (15) days?
Then the permit holder can submit a written request for an extension of up to thirty (30) additional days.

How long can a pharmacy be operated without a pharmacist manager?
Up to fifteen (15) days, *unless* the pharmacy obtains an extension from the Board.

Can a pharmacist serve as the pharmacist manager of more than one pharmacy at a time?
No.

> **EXCEPTION:** If a permit holder loses the services of a pharmacist manager and is unable to obtain a suitable replacement, then he/she may apply for a waiver. This waiver allows a pharmacist manager to manage more than one pharmacy for up to sixty (60) days beyond the initial fifteen (15)-day period.

PHARMACY TECHNICIANS

TRUE OR FALSE
A pharmacy technician must work under the direct supervision of another pharmacy technician.
False. A pharmacy technician must work under the direct, immediate, personal supervision of a pharmacist.

What are some duties that may be performed by a pharmacy technician?
- Carry containers of drugs in and around the pharmacy.
- Count tablets and capsules and place them in a container.
- Type and print labels.
- Maintain pharmacy records.
- Assist the pharmacist in preparing and reconstituting drugs.
- Enter information into a patient profile.
- Place drug orders.

When a pharmacy technician finishes preparing a parenteral product, what must occur prior to dispensing?
The supervising pharmacist must initial the label of the product to document final inspection and to accept total responsibility for its preparation.

Pharmacy technicians can never…
- Accept prescription orders placed verbally (e.g. by telephone).
- Set foot in the pharmacy when a pharmacist is not on duty.
- Perform any act requiring independent professional judgment.
- Perform a duty without a written protocol.
- Perform a duty without being trained.

BUILDING STANDARDS

What is the minimum size requirement for the prescription area of a pharmacy?
Two hundred fifty (250) square feet.

What is the minimum size of the prescription working counter?
The answer depends on the number of pharmacists on duty simultaneously. See below.

- One (1) pharmacist on duty: 10 ft. x 2 ft.
- Two (2) pharmacists on duty simultaneously: 10 ft. x 2 ft.
- Three (3) pharmacists on duty simultaneously: 15 ft. x 2 ft.
- Four (4) pharmacists on duty simultaneously: 20 ft. x 2 ft.
- Five (5) pharmacists on duty simultaneously: 25 ft. x 2 ft.
- Six (6) pharmacists on duty simultaneously: 30 ft. x 2 ft.

Note: 10 ft. x 2 ft. for up to 2 pharmacists *plus* 5 ft. of length for each additional pharmacist working at once.

Do minimum space requirements apply to central fill pharmacies?
No.

For pharmacies located inside retail establishments with different hours, you should give special consideration to what aspect of construction?
Security. The pharmacy must be equipped with a barrier device that reaches from floor to ceiling.

What feature must the barrier device possess?
It must be impenetrable by hand or a reach extender.

When must a pharmacy be locked?
Whenever a licensed pharmacist is not present in the immediate building.

Where must the hours of the pharmacy be posted?
At all points of public access.

When can the pharmacy be accessed by a non-pharmacist?
Only for true emergencies (e.g. fires, natural disasters, police matters).

If the pharmacy is accessed by a non-pharmacist, then who must be notified?
The pharmacist manager.

What medications must be stored in a locked compartment (e.g. cabinet or safe)?
Schedule I medications must be stored in a locked compartment. Other controlled substances *may* be store in a locked compartment.

If Schedule II – V controlled substances are not stored in a locked compartment, how must they be stored?
Dispersed throughout the stock of non-controlled substances in a manner that obstructs theft.

At minimum, how many telephones must be accessible in the prescription area of a pharmacy?
One (1).

How many sinks must be in the prescription area of a pharmacy?
One (1).

Note: There must be at least one (1) sink in the prescription area that is solely for pharmaceutical purposes.

The sink must have ____ and ____ running water.
- ✓ Hot.
- ✓ Cold.

TRUE OR FALSE
There must be a restroom in the prescription area.
False. Restrooms must be reasonably close to, but outside of, the prescription area.

You must work on Super Bowl Sunday. You know that no televisions are allowed in the pharmacy, so you position a TV outside of the pharmacy to watch the game. Is this legally permitted?
No. A television cannot be situated for viewing from the prescription area, regardless of where it is located.

The store manager asks you if she can use a shelf in the pharmacy to store overstock candy bars. She has no other place to put them. How should you respond?
Tell the manager that the prescription area cannot be used to store items other than those used in preparation, dispensing, or delivery of drugs.

You are working with a part-time floater pharmacist today. She is working a 12-hour shift. She could not find anyone to watch her cat, so she brings her cat to work. What should you tell her?
Animals are not allowed in the pharmacy.

> **Note:** Animals are only allowed in pharmacies for security reasons.

TRUE OR FALSE
Personnel may enter the pharmacy to clean, deliver, or perform other necessary functions only when a pharmacist is present.
True.

APPROVAL OF PLANS

TRUE OR FALSE
Before beginning construction on a new pharmacy, floor plans must be submitted to the Board for approval.
True.

TRUE OR FALSE
You are not required to submit floor plans for Board approval when moving an existing pharmacy to a new location.
False.

After the floor plans are submitted to the Board, how long does it take to receive the approval or denial?
Up to ninety (90) days.

When submitting floor plans to the Board, must you include dimensions (i.e. measurements)?
Yes.

Can you continue to operate a pharmacy during renovations?
No, *unless* you receive approval from the Board.

How do you obtain approval from the Board to operate a pharmacy during renovations?
Take safety precautions to protect the employees and customers, then submit the plans for renovation and a description of the safety precautions at least thirty (30) days before the renovation work is scheduled to begin.

If approved, will the Board contact you?
No. If you do not hear from the Board within thirty (30) days, then you can proceed as planned. You will only hear from the Board if there is an objection to the plan.

SANITARY STANDARDS

What are the sanitary standards that apply to pharmacies?
Pharmacies must be...
- ✓ Dry.
- ✓ Clean.
- ✓ Orderly.
- ✓ Well ventilated.
- ✓ Free from rodents and insects.
- ✓ Well lighted.

Are there any sanitary standards for the *people* working in a pharmacy?
Yes. Everyone working in the prescription area must maintain a clean and professional appearance.

SUPPLIES

Each pharmacy must maintain a supply of _____ and _____ adequate to meet the needs of the health profession and patients they intend to serve.
- ✓ Drugs.
- ✓ Devices.

When applying for a pharmacy permit, the applicant must prove to the Board that he/she has ordered (or currently possesses) and will continue to maintain an inventory appropriate for the pharmacy. How does an applicant prove this?
By submitting an affidavit to the Board.

> **Note:** An affidavit is a sworn statement made in writing and certified by an officer of the law.

What is the *minimum* amount of inventory a pharmacy must maintain?
Prescription drugs and devices from a wholesaler or manufacturer valued at $5,000.

> **Note:** The minimum inventory requirement does *not* apply to central fill facilities.

Can a pharmacy *ever* allow their inventory to drop below the $5,000 minimum described above?
No, **unless** it is a central fill pharmacy, in which case the minimum inventory requirement does not apply.

Which drugs must be removed from stock?
- ✓ Expired drugs.
- ✓ Drugs not meeting the legal standards for strength and purity.
- ✓ Drugs with strength and purity different from that stated on the label.
- ✓ Improperly stored drugs.
- ✓ Deteriorated drugs.
- ✓ Drugs that are unfit, misbranded, or adulterated.

Who is ultimately responsible for ensuring these drugs are removed from stock?
The pharmacist manager.

Once removed from active stock, can these drugs be sold or given away?
No. The pharmacy must dispose of the drugs *or* return them to the wholesaler or manufacturer for disposal.

Prior to disposing of a controlled substance, who must be contacted?
The nearest DEA office must be contacted for permission and instructions on how to dispose of the controlled substance.

When disposing of a controlled substance, what information must be recorded?
- ✓ Name of the controlled substance.
- ✓ Quantity of the substance.
- ✓ Date of disposal.
- ✓ Method of disposal.

EQUIPMENT

What are the minimum equipment requirements for pharmacies?
- ✓ A refrigerator with a thermometer (for drug storage only).
- ✓ Prescription files.
- ✓ A current copy of the Pennsylvania Pharmacy Act.
- ✓ A current copy of Chapter 27 of Pennsylvania Code.
- ✓ Federal and state statutes and regulations for pharmacy practice.
- ✓ Tools needed to prepare and dispense prescriptions.
- ✓ An adequate reference library.

Note: These equipment requirements do *not* apply to central fill facilities.

The reference library must accomplish the following:
- ✓ Enables safe and proper dispensing of medications.
- ✓ Covers the technical, clinical and professional aspects of pharmacy.
- ✓ Enables safe and effective compounding of medications.
- ✓ Lists possible side effects and adverse effects of medications.
- ✓ Lists therapeutic equivalents for medications.
- ✓ Provides guidelines for counseling patients.
- ✓ Includes the latest editions and current supplements of reference sources.
- ✓ Relates to the specialization of the pharmacy.

PHARMACIST BREAKS

If only one (1) pharmacist is on duty, can that pharmacist take a break?
Yes, for up to thirty (30) minutes.

TRUE OR FALSE
A pharmacist must be present at all times when the prescription area is open.
True.

Can the pharmacy remain open while the pharmacist is on break?
Yes, *if* the pharmacist remains in the pharmacy or in the immediate building where the pharmacy is located.

Note: If the pharmacy is open while the pharmacist is on break, then the pharmacist must remain available for emergencies or counseling upon request.

If the pharmacy is in a complex that houses other businesses, such as a mall, can the pharmacy remain open while the pharmacist visits another business in the complex?
No.

What can pharmacy technicians do during a pharmacist's break?
- ✓ Accept new prescriptions.
- ✓ Prepare prescriptions for final verification by the pharmacist.
- ✓ Sell prescriptions that have been verified by the pharmacist.

PHARMACY PRACTICE

What activities are included in the scope of pharmacy practice?
- ✓ Interpretation, evaluation, and implementation of prescriptions or medical orders to provide pharmacy services.
- ✓ Delivery, dispensing, or distribution of prescription drugs.
- ✓ Involvement in drug and device selection.
- ✓ Drug regimen review.
- ✓ Drug administration.
- ✓ Drug or drug-related research.
- ✓ Compounding.
- ✓ Storage of drugs and devices.
- ✓ Managing drug therapy.
- ✓ Maintaining records.
- ✓ Patient counseling.
- ✓ Other functions involved in providing these services.

What is a nonproprietary drug?
A drug product that can only be obtained by prescription.

What is a proprietary drug?
A drug that can be sold without a prescription.

STANDARDS OF PRACTICE

When dispensing new prescriptions, the pharmacist can use one (1) of two (2) containers. What are the two (2) containers?
A new and clean container *or* the manufacturer's original container.

TRUE OR FALSE
When refilling a prescription, the pharmacist can reuse the container from the previous fill.
True, *if* the container is clean and reusable.

Note: Although the container may be reused, the Poison Prevention Packaging Act prohibits the reuse of child safety caps. Therefore, a new child safety cap must be provided with each refill. Additionally, a new label must be affixed to the container, regardless of whether the container is new or reused.

What information must be included in the prescription files for non-controlled substance medications?
- Name and address of patient.
- Name and address of prescriber.
- Date the prescription was issued (for controlled substance prescriptions and prescriptions with PRN refills).
- Name and quantity of drug prescribed.
- Directions for use.
- Cautions for the ultimate user (e.g. auxiliary labels).
- Date the prescription was compounded and dispensed.
- Name or initials of the dispensing pharmacist.

Note: For controlled substance prescriptions, the prescriber's DEA number must also be included.

What can a prescriber use to issue Schedule II controlled substance prescriptions?
- Ink.
- Indelible pencil.
- Typewriter.
- Word processor.
- Computer printer.
- By electronic means.

Note: C-II prescriptions must be manually signed by the prescriber; however, electronic signatures are acceptable for C-II e-prescriptions.

When a prescription is refilled, what information must be included in the pharmacy records?
- Date of refill.
- Name or initials of the dispensing pharmacist.
- Quantity dispensed.

Note: If dispensing a quantity other than the quantity prescribed, you must indicate the changes on the back of the prescription or enter the changes in the computerized files.

How long must a pharmacy maintain an original prescription (or an image of the original prescription)?
For two (2) years from the date of the most recent filling.

Is it legal to maintain an *image* of the prescription, rather than the original prescription itself, for recordkeeping purposes?
Yes.

Note: The original prescriptions *or* prescription image must be maintained in a readily retrievable fashion.

When should a pharmacist decline to fill (or refill) a prescription?
The pharmacist knows or has reason to know that the prescription is:
- False.
- Fraudulent.
- Unlawful.
- Covered by a third-party who will not provide reimbursement.
- For use by a person other than for whom it was prescribed.
- Going to be diverted, abused, or misused.
- Not in the best interest of the patient.

What information must appear on the label affixed to the container of a prescription drug or device?
- ✓ Name, address, phone number, and DEA number of the pharmacy.
- ✓ Name of the patient.
- ✓ Directions for use.
- ✓ Name of the prescriber.
- ✓ Serial number of the prescription (Rx number).
- ✓ Date originally filled.
- ✓ Trade or brand name of the drug.
- ✓ Strength and dosage form.
- ✓ Quantity dispensed.
- ✓ Manufacturer's name or a suitable abbreviation (for generic drugs only).
- ✓ The statement: "Caution: Federal law prohibits the transfer of this drug to any person other than the patient for whom it was prescribed." (controlled substances only)

Do these prescription label requirements apply when dispensing medication in an institutional setting?
No, not for drugs dispensed in unit dose packaging.

In an institutional setting, when a drug is *not* dispensed in unit dose packaging, what information must appear on the label?
- ✓ Patient Name.
- ✓ Drug Name.
- ✓ Drug Strength.
- ✓ Dosing instructions.
- ✓ Lot number.

What information must be included on the label of parenteral, enteral, or total parenteral nutrition products?
- ✓ Patient Name.
- ✓ Ingredients (including name, strength, and quantity).
- ✓ Diluent.
- ✓ Pharmacist's initials.

When can a pharmacist dispense a Schedule V controlled substance *without* a prescription?
Yes, if the following criteria are met:
- ⇨ Must be dispensed by a pharmacist (financial transaction may be completed by a non-pharmacist).
- ⇨ Maximum of 8 ounces (240 mL) of opium-containing C-V within a 72-hour period **and** maximum of 4 ounces (120 mL) of any other C-V within a 72-hour period.
- ⇨ Purchaser must be at least 18 years of age.
- ⇨ If unknown to the pharmacist, the purchaser must furnish identification that includes proof of age.
- ⇨ Pharmacist must maintain a bound record book to record the dispensing of C-V products without a prescription. The following information must be record in the book:
    - o Purchaser's name and address.
    - o Name and quantity of controlled substance sold.
    - o Date of each sale.
    - o Name of initials of dispensing pharmacist.

Note: C-V narcotic cough medications ***cannot*** be sold in Pennsylvania without a prescription.

Narcotic C-V medications must have a label affixed to the bottle or container at the time of sale that includes…
- ✓ The name and address of the pharmacy.
- ✓ The initials of the pharmacist.
- ✓ The date of sale.

TRUE OR FALSE
A pharmacist can sell C-V narcotic *cough* medications (e.g. containing codeine) to individuals without a prescription.
False per Pennsylvania Code Title 49 §27.18(f)

> **Note:** This rule does not apply to C-V cough preparations used within an institution, such as a hospital.

TRUE OR FALSE
You may fill or refill a prescription if you know the prescriber is no longer in practice (e.g. retired, deceased).
False.

TRUE OR FALSE
Prescriptions for non-controlled substances *never* expire.
False. Per Pennsylvania Code, non-controlled substance prescriptions expire one (1) year after the date written

What does it mean when a prescriber authorizes "ad lib" or "PRN" refills?
The patient is entitled to refills for a period of one (1) year.

When do prescriptions for C-II controlled substances expire?
Six (6) months after the date written.

When can you refill a prescription for a C-II controlled substance?
Never.

What are the limits for C-III, C-IV, and C-V controlled substance refills?
- ✓ A prescriber cannot authorize more than 5 refills.
- ✓ The prescription and refills expire 6 months after the date written.

> **Note:** Federal law does *not* impose the 5-refill limit/6-month expiration date on C-V controlled substance prescriptions. In this case, Pennsylvania law is more restrictive. Remember, when federal and state law differ, the more restrictive law prevails.

Is it legal to pre-pack and pre-label convenient quantities of a medication for future use?
Yes, *if* done under the direct supervision of a registered pharmacist.

What information must appear on the label of a pre-packed medication?
- ✓ Drug name.
- ✓ Manufacturer's name (for generic drugs only).
- ✓ Drug strength.
- ✓ Manufacturer's lot number.
- ✓ Expiration date (if any).

The pharmacy must maintain a log to record the information outlined above. What other information must be included in the log?
- ✓ The date of pre-packing.
- ✓ The quantity of medication pre-packed.

Who can receive and transcribe oral orders (e.g. telephone prescriptions)?
- ✓ Registered pharmacists.
- ✓ Pharmacy interns.

> **Note:** Pharmacy interns must be under the direct, immediate and personal supervision of a pharmacist.

TRUE OR FALSE
Oral orders must be reduced to writing *immediately*.
True.

In an institutional setting, when can a pharmacist compound, prepare, dispense, fill, sell, or give away a drug?
Only after receiving a prescription or medication order (or a direct copy of the original prescription or medication order).

A cash-paying patient continually requests unreasonably early refills for his atenolol. What should you tell the patient?
Pennsylvania law only allows me to refill prescriptions at a reasonable time prior to the time when the contents of the prescription should be consumed according to the prescriber's instructions.

GENERIC SUBSTITUTION

How do you determine whether a drug is generically equivalent to a brand drug?
Generic equivalent drugs are *A-rated* in the Orange Book.

What is the official title of the Orange Book?
Approved Drug Products with Therapeutic Equivalence Evaluations.

When you receive a prescription for a brand name medication, you must substitute a _____ unless requested otherwise by the customer or indicated otherwise by the prescriber.
Less expensive, generically equivalent drug.

> **Note:** Narrow therapeutic index (NTI) drugs are an exception.

If a prescriber wants the brand drug to be dispensed, what words must appear on the face of the prescription?
Brand necessary *or* brand medically necessary.

A prescription For Lipitor® is submitted orally. Should you dispense brand Lipitor or the generic equivalent, atorvastatin?
Atorvastatin. You only dispense the brand name drug if the prescriber (or his/her agent) expressly says the brand name is necessary and substitution is not allowed.

TRUE OR FALSE
All pharmacies must clearly post a sign to notify the public that prescriptions are subject to generic substitution unless otherwise directed by the patient or prescriber.
True. The sign must read "Pennsylvania law permits pharmacists to substitute a less expensive generically equivalent drug for a prescribed brand name dug unless you or your physician direct otherwise." The text on the sign must be in bold letters not less than 1 inch in height on a white background.

What else must be clearly posted in a way that is easily accessible to the public?
A list of commonly used generic equivalent drugs and interchangeable biological products containing the generic or nonproprietary names and brand names (where applicable). Additionally, each pharmacy must have a price listing of brand name and generic equivalent drug products and interchangeable biological products publically available at the pharmacy for selection by the customer.

When can pharmacists substitute an interchangeable biological product for a prescribed biological product?
- ✓ The FDA has determined that the products are interchangeable.
- ✓ The prescriber does not indicate (verbally or in writing) that substitution is prohibited.
- ✓ The person presenting the prescription is notified of substitution with the retail price difference and informed that they may refuse substitution.

When an *interchangeable biological product* is dispensed, the prescriber must be notified within _____.
Seventy-two (72) hours.

> **Note:** Prescriber notification is *not* required when dispensing refills of the same product.

TRUE OR FALSE
Substitution with a less expensive generic equivalent is contingent upon whether the pharmacy has the brand name drug or a generic equivalent drug in stock.
True.

Can a pharmacist be held liable for any negative effects (e.g. damage, injury, death) caused by dispensing a generic substitute or interchangeable biological product?
No, *unless* the drug or biological product was improperly substituted.

NARROW THERAPEUTIC INDEX DRUGS

TRUE OR FALSE
A narrow therapeutic index (NTI) drug is not substitutable regardless of its bioequivalency rating in the Orange Book.
True.

What is the definition of a narrow therapeutic index drug?
A drug that requires careful titration and patient monitoring to achieve safe and effective use, and one of the two following criteria must apply:

- There is less than a two (2)-fold difference between the median lethal dose (LD50) and the median effective dose (ED50).
- There is less than a two (2)-fold difference between the minimum toxic concentration and the minimum effective concentration.

Does the FDA or the Pennsylvania Board of Pharmacy publish a current list of NTI drugs?
No.

Which drugs possess a narrow therapeutic index?
As established in the previous question-and-answer, no current list of NTI drugs has been published; however, in 1988 the FDA published a *sample list* of NTI drugs. See below for a summary of that list.

✓ Aminophylline	✓ Isoethrine Mesylate	✓ Prazosin
✓ Carbamazepine	✓ Isoproterenol	✓ Primidone
✓ Clindamycin	✓ Levoxyine	✓ Procainamide
✓ Clonidine	✓ Lithium Carbonate	✓ Quinidine
✓ Digoxin	✓ Metaproterenol	✓ Theophylline
✓ Disopyramide	✓ Minoxidil	✓ Valproic Acid
✓ Dyphylline	✓ Oxytriphylline	✓ Valproate Sodium
✓ Guanethidine	✓ Phenytoin	✓ Warfarin

Note: The Pennsylvania Generic Substitution Law urges pharmacists to utilize a variety of sources and their professional training to determine whether a specific drug is an NTI drug, so do not rely solely on this list.

PROSPECTIVE DRUG REVIEW

As a pharmacist, must you perform prospective drug reviews (PDR) for every new prescription, *or* just the prescriptions for patients with multiple disease states?
You must perform a prospective drug review for *every* new prescription.

TRUE OR FALSE
Prospective drug reviews are *not* required when dispensing medication orders in an institutional setting.
False.

What is the purpose of a prospective drug review?
To assure that use of the drug as prescribed is not likely to have an adverse medical outcome.

What potential problems do you look for when performing a prospective drug review?
- ✓ Therapeutic duplications.
- ✓ Drug-drug interactions.
- ✓ Incorrect dosage.
- ✓ Incorrect duration of therapy.
- ✓ Drug-allergy interactions.
- ✓ Clinical abuse or misuse.

What action must you take after discovering a potential problem?
Intervene and attempt to resolve the problem.

Are physicians required to conduct prospective drug reviews when dispensing prescriptions from an Emergency Department (ED)?
No.

Aside from ED dispensing, in what other scenarios is a prospective drug review *not* required.
- ✓ When a medical practitioner dispenses a drug.
- ✓ When dispensing a drug to a medical practitioner who will administer the drug.
- ✓ When dispensing a radiopharmaceutical to a physician who will administer the drug.

PATIENT PROFILES

What information should be collected and maintained in a patient profile?
1. Patient demographics.
    a. Name.
    b. Address.
    c. Phone number.
    d. Date of birth (or age).
    e. Gender.
2. Individual history.
    a. Allergies and drug reactions.
    b. Current medications and devices.
3. Pharmacist's comments regarding drug therapy.

What is the pharmacist's responsibility regarding patient profiles?
To make a reasonable effort to collect pertinent information on each patient.

Is a pharmacist required to obtain information when the patient or caregiver refuses to provide it?
No.

How long must pharmacies maintain patient profiles?
For two (2) years from the date of the most recent entry.

TRUE OR FALSE
Patient profiles are public record.
False. Patient profiles are confidential.

When can a pharmacist reveal information from the pharmacy records?
- Patient consent is obtained.
- The Board requires the information for a proceeding.
- State or Federal law or regulations permit disclosure.
- Court order.

COUNSELING

When must a pharmacist offer counseling?
Each time a new prescription is dispensed in an outpatient setting.

Is an offer to counsel required when dispensing to inpatients?
No.

If the patient's caregiver (e.g. spouse, home nurse) picks up the prescription, are you required to make the offer to counsel to the caregiver?
Yes.

Must the pharmacist be the person to extend the offer to counsel?
No. The pharmacist can designate someone else to make the offer (e.g. the cashier).

How should the offer to counsel be made?
Orally, unless the pharmacist determines that a written offer would be more effective (e.g. the patient is hearing-impaired).

When prescriptions are delivered to a patient's home, it is not possible to counsel in-person. In these cases, how should the pharmacist provide counseling?
By telephone.

When dispensing prescriptions by mail, the person delivering the medication to the patient's home is not an employee of the pharmacy. In these cases, how should the offer to counsel be made?
By telephone or by sending a written offer to counsel with a toll-free number.

Aside from a pharmacist, who can counsel patients/caregivers?
No one. Only a pharmacist can provide counseling.

Must a pharmacist provide counseling if the patient or caregiver refuses the offer to counsel?
No.

What information may be discussed during counseling?
- Name and description of the medication.
- Dosage form and route of administration.
- Duration of therapy.
- Special directions and precautions.
- Common severe side effects, interactions, and contraindications the patient may encounter, including how to avoid them and what action to take if they occur.
- Self-monitoring techniques.
- Storage instructions.
- Refill information.
- Action to take in the event of a missed dose.

What if you extend an offer to counsel and the patient or caregiver does not respond?
Failure to respond is equivalent to refusal.

What must be done when a patient refuses counseling?
The refusal must be documented.

Who documents the refusal?
The person who extended the offer.

How should the refusal be documented?
By making a note on the original prescription, in the patient profile, or in the electronic records, *or* by maintaining a statement of refusal signed by the patient or caregiver. The documentation must also include the name or initials of the person recording the refusal.

CENTRAL FILL PHARMACIES

What tasks can be completed by central fill pharmacies (or central prescription processing centers)?
- ✓ Prescription processing.
- ✓ Prescription filling.
- ✓ Prescription refilling.
- ✓ Delivering processed, filled, or refills prescriptions to a dispensing/delivering pharmacy.

What relationship must exist between a central fill pharmacy and the originating pharmacy?
They must have a contract or share the same owner.

What provisions must be included in the contract?
Provisions for protecting the confidentiality of patient information.

Which pharmacy name, address, phone number, and DEA number should appear on the label of the prescription bottle when a central fill pharmacy is used?
The pharmacy that dispenses the prescription.

Pharmacies that use central fill facilities must have _____.
Operating policies and procedures that include an audit trail.

What is the purpose of an audit trail?
To record and document the process and the people accountable at each step in the process.

TRUE OR FALSE
Pharmacies using a central fill facility do *not* need to share a common electronic file with the central facility.
False. The pharmacies must share a common electronic file.

Which pharmacy is responsible for properly filling each prescription?
Both pharmacies.

Which pharmacy is responsible for making the offer to counsel?
The pharmacy that dispenses the prescription.

Central fill pharmacies are exempt from certain requirements. What are the exemptions?
- ✓ Exempt from the minimum pharmacy size requirements.
- ✓ Exempt from the requirement to have a sink in the prescription area.
- ✓ Exempt from maintaining an inventory of at least $5,000 worth of prescription drugs and devices.

MAILING PRESCRIPTIONS

What method(s) can be used for mailing prescriptions?
First-class mail *or* a common carrier.

Note: Slower means can be used only if the purchaser agrees.

TRUE OR FALSE
Reconstituted antibiotics *cannot* be dispensed via the mail.
True.

Can you mail prescriptions that are subject to significant deterioration by heat, cold, or prolonged agitation?
Yes, *if* you ship the prescriptions in a manner that preserves their integrity.

CONTROLLED SUBSTANCES

CONTROLLED SUBSTANCE CHARACTERISTICS BY SCHEDULE

SCHEDULE I CONTROLLED SUBSTANCES

- ✓ High abuse potential.
- ✓ No accepted medical use.
- ✓ Lacks safety.

SCHEDULE II CONTROLLED SUBSTANCES

- ✓ High potential for abuse.
- ✓ Accepted medical use.
- ✓ Severe potential for physical/psychological dependence.

SCHEDULE III CONTROLLED SUBSTANCES

- ✓ Moderate abuse potential.
- ✓ Accepted medical use.
- ✓ Moderate-low potential for dependence.

SCHEDULE IV CONTROLLED SUBSTANCES

- ✓ Mild abuse potential.
- ✓ Accepted medical use.
- ✓ Mild potential for physical/psychological dependence.

SCHEDULE V CONTROLLED SUBSTANCES

- ✓ Low abuse potential.
- ✓ Accepted medical use.
- ✓ Low potential for physical/psychological dependence.
- ✓ May be sold in Pennsylvania without a prescription (excluding C-V narcotic cough preparations).
    - ⇨ Must be dispensed by a pharmacist (financial transaction may be completed by a non-pharmacist).
    - ⇨ Maximum of 8 ounces (240 mL) of an opium-containing C-V within a 72-hour period *and* maximum of 4 ounces (120 mL) of a non-opium C-V within a 72-hour period.
    - ⇨ Purchaser must be at least 18 years of age.
    - ⇨ If unknown to the pharmacist, the purchaser must furnish identification that includes proof of age.
    - ⇨ Pharmacist must maintain a bound record book to record the dispensing of C-V products without a prescription. The following information must be record in the book:
        - o Purchaser's name and address.
        - o Name and quantity of controlled substance sold.
        - o Date of sale.
        - o Name of initials of dispensing pharmacist.

Who is required to maintain controlled substance inventory records?
- ✓ Manufacturers.
- ✓ Distributors.
- ✓ Dispensers (pharmacies).

> **Note:** Essentially, every business that touches a controlled substance must maintain inventory records.

A patient insists that you dispense sixty (60) tablets of his controlled substance medication, but the doctor only wrote for thirty (30) tablets with two (2) refills. Is there any way you can dispense sixty (60) tablets?
Only if you receive authorization from the doctor to dispense more than the written quantity. The same is also true for psychiatric medications.

> **Note:** Document any changes on the prescription hard copy (i.e. Okay to dispense #60 per Dr. Jones on 5/31/17 and include your signature or initials).

Can anabolic steroids be prescribed to enhance performance in exercise, sports, or games?
No.

Can anabolic steroids be prescribed to increase muscle mass, strength, or weight?
No, **unless** it is medically necessary.

Can a physician's secretary submit C-II controlled substance prescriptions verbally (i.e. over the telephone)?
No.

> **Note:** In emergencies, a prescriber can verbally order a C-II controlled substance. The prescriber must **personally** call the pharmacy. The pharmacist must reduce the verbal prescription to writing immediately. The quantity must be limited to the amount necessary to treat the patient for the emergency period. Furthermore, the prescriber must furnish a hand-signed prescription within seventy-two (72) hours.

If a prescriber fails to furnish a hand-signed prescription within seventy-two (72) hours, how must the pharmacist respond?
The pharmacist must notify the nearest DEA office.

An emergency C-II prescription is only appropriate if _____ administration of the controlled substance is necessary for proper treatment, and _____ is available.
- ✓ Immediate.
- ✓ No appropriate alternative.

TRUE OR FALSE
Schedule II controlled substance prescriptions must be kept in a file separate from all other pharmacy records.
True.

What are the options for filing C-III, C-IV, and C-V controlled substance prescriptions?
C-III, C-IV, and C-V prescriptions can either be filed separate from all other pharmacy records **or** filed together with non-controlled substance prescriptions.

> **Note:** If C-III, C-IV, and C-V prescriptions are filed together with non-controlled substance prescriptions, then they must be marked with a "C" in **red ink** no less than one (1) inch high.

NEEDLES AND SYRINGES

TRUE OR FALSE
Hypodermic needles and syringes can be sold *without* a prescription.
True.

Where must hypodermic needles and syringes be stored?
Behind the pharmacy counter.

ELECTRONIC PRESCRIBING

In addition to the information that must appear on a *written* prescription, what additional information must be included on an electronic prescription?
- ✓ Prescriber's telephone number.
- ✓ Date of transmission.
- ✓ Name of pharmacy intended to receive the prescription.

Note: Electronic signatures are permitted, and electronic prescriptions must be sent using means designed to prevent access by unauthorized individuals (e.g. encryption).

TRUE OR FALSE
The pharmacy must maintain a hard copy of electronic prescriptions for two (2) years from the date of most recent filling.
False. It is true that the record must be maintained for two (2) years from the date of most recent filling, **but** either a hard copy **or** a readily retrievable image can be used for recordkeeping purposes.

Remember that pharmacies are prohibited from supplying prescribers with fax machines to fax prescriptions?
Pharmacies are also prohibited from supplying prescribers with electronic equipment to transmit e-prescriptions.

Per Pennsylvania legislation, which medications can be issued by e-prescription?
Non-controlled substances **and** Schedule II, III, IV, and V controlled substances. In other words, e-prescriptions are now regarded as being equivalent to written prescription orders.

Does current legislation allow Schedule II controlled substance prescriptions to be issued electronically?
Yes.

What DEA requirement must be met before a prescriber can issue and a pharmacy can dispense controlled substance e-prescriptions?
The application (i.e. software) used by the pharmacy must be certified by an approved certification body in compliance with DEA requirements.

Why does the DEA impose special software requirements for prescribers and pharmacies who issue and dispense controlled substance e-prescriptions?
To prevent fraudulent electronic controlled substance prescriptions from being written and dispensed.

FAX MACHINES

TRUE OR FALSE
You can fill a faxed prescription for a Schedule II controlled substance.
True, **but** only if the original prescription (hand-signed by the prescriber) is presented to the pharmacist prior to dispensing. The original, hand-signed prescription must be maintained in the pharmacy records.

Note: There are three (3) cases in which a faxed C-II prescription can serve as the original prescription.

What are the three (3) cases in which a faxed C-II prescription can serve as the original prescription?
1. Home infusion patients (assuming it is an injectable preparation).
2. Long-term care patients.
3. Hospice patients.

Is faxing a valid method of transmitting prescriptions for non-controlled substances?
Yes.

Is faxing a valid method of transmitting prescriptions for C-III, C-IV, and C-V controlled substances?
Yes.

Can the faxed copy of a non-controlled substance or a C-III, C-IV, or C-V controlled substance prescription be used as the original prescription for recordkeeping purposes?
Yes.

How long are pharmacies required to maintain copies of faxed prescriptions?
Two (2) years.

You want the local medical offices to send their prescriptions by fax. Can you offer to give them a fax machine?
No. A pharmacy **cannot** contribute to the installation of a fax machine in a prescriber's office or at an institution.

PRESCRIPTION TRANSFERS

When a prescription is transferred from your pharmacy to another pharmacy, you must cancel the original prescription and record what information?
- ✓ The name of the pharmacy where the prescription was transferred.
- ✓ The date of transfer.
- ✓ The name or initials of the transferring pharmacist.

What information must be recorded by the pharmacist who receives the transferred prescription?
- ✓ Notation indicating the prescription is a transfer.
- ✓ The date the original prescription was written.
- ✓ The date the original prescription was first filled along with the refill record.
- ✓ The original number of refills authorized.
- ✓ The number of valid refills remaining.
- ✓ The location and Rx number of the original prescription.
- ✓ The name of the pharmacy and the pharmacist that gave the transfer.

Can you transfer Schedule II controlled substance prescriptions?
No.

EMERGENCY REFILLS

When is it appropriate to dispense an emergency refill?
The patient is out of refills and the drug is essential to the maintenance of life.

What must occur prior to dispensing an emergency refill?
You must first attempt to obtain a refill authorization from the prescriber.

Can you dispense an emergency refill for a controlled substance?
No.

> **Note:** Remember, you may dispense an *emergency prescription* for a C-II upon oral order from a prescriber.

How much medication can you dispense in an emergency refill?
A seventy-two (72)-hour supply.

Can you dispense more than one (1) emergency refill?
No.

After you dispense an emergency refill, when must you notify the prescriber that the dispensing occurred?
Within seventy-two (72) hours.

PRESCRIPTION COPIES

TRUE OR FALSE
Patients have the right to request a copy of an original prescription.
True.

What must be clearly indicated on the face of a copied prescription?
That it is a copy and it may not be used to obtain a new prescription or a refill.

Is there anything you, as the pharmacist, must do prior to furnishing the patient with a copy of a prescription?
Yes. You must obtain authorization (if an agent of the patient is picking up the copy) and identification, such as a driver's license.

When furnishing a prescription copy, must you document the action?
Yes. The following information must be recorded:
- ✓ Date the copy was furnished.
- ✓ Name of the patient (or agent of the patient) receiving the copy.
- ✓ Name of the person giving the copy to the patient (or agent of the patient).

RETURNING UNDELIVERED MEDICATION TO STOCK

TRUE OR FALSE
Once a medication leaves the pharmacy, it cannot be returned to stock.
True.

TRUE OR FALSE
Prescriptions that have *not* left the control of the pharmacy may be returned to stock.
True.

You are returning a prescription to stock since the patient has not picked up the medication in several days. You notice there is a stock bottle with enough space to hold the tablets from the prescription you are returning. The NDC numbers match. Should you pour the tablets from the prescription bottle into the stock bottle?
No, *unless* there is a way to confirm that the medications share the same lot number and expiration date.

Why are lot numbers important?
In the case of a recall, lot numbers are used to identify affected batches of medication.

When can you *safely* return a medication to a stock bottle?
Only when the pharmacy tracks all medications by lot number and expiration date.

After returning a prescription to stock, when must you dispense the medication?
Within six (6) months from the date the drug was originally prepared for dispensing, assuming you do not know the lot number and expiration date.

During a manufacturer or FDA recall, how must you treat medication in a container with *no* lot number?
Assume that it is included in the recall and follow the recall procedure.

COMPUTERIZED RECORDKEEPING

How quickly must a pharmacy's computer system retrieve information from all prescriptions filled over the previous twelve (12) months?
Immediately.

How quickly must a pharmacy's computer system retrieve information from all prescriptions filled over the previous twenty-four (24) months?
Within three (3) working days.

If the pharmacy's computerized recordkeeping system stops working temporarily and prescriptions are processed manually, when must the information be entered in the computerized recordkeeping system?
As soon as the system is available.

RELIGIOUS, MORAL, OR ETHICAL OBJECTIONS TO FILLING

When first hired, a pharmacist should _____ if his beliefs will limit the drug products he will dispense.
Take steps to notify the owner and pharmacist manager.

TRUE OR FALSE
An employer can terminate a pharmacist for refusing to fill certain prescriptions based on religious, moral, or ethical beliefs.
False. The owner and manager should provide reasonable accommodations that respect the pharmacist's choice while assuring patient service.

TRUE OR FALSE
If you object to the filling of a prescription, you must not interfere with another pharmacist's decision to fill the prescription.
True.

COLLABORATIVE DRUG THERAPY MANAGEMENT

What is the key difference between collaborative drug therapy management agreements and drug therapy protocols?
- ✓ Collaborative drug therapy management agreements are used in outpatient settings.
- ✓ Drug therapy protocols are used in inpatient settings.

Must collaborative drug therapy agreements be in writing?
Yes, and the written agreement must be signed and dated by the participating physician and pharmacist.

Pharmacists who manage drug therapy pursuant to a collaborative drug therapy agreement must possess professional liability insurance. How much coverage do they need?
Minimum coverage in the amount of $1,000,000 per occurrence or claims made.

TRUE OR FALSE
A pharmacist can provide an economic incentive to a physician in return for participating in a collaborative drug therapy agreement.
False.

TRUE OR FALSE
A pharmacist who is employed by a physician under a collaborative agreement to manage drug therapy may also engage in retail dispensing while in the health care practice or within the context of employment.
False.

TRUE OR FALSE
A pharmacist providing drug therapy management *cannot* have access to patient records.
False. The pharmacist must have access to patient records when providing drug therapy management.

What drug therapy management decisions does a pharmacist have the authority to make in a collaborative drug therapy agreement or protocol?
Within the limits of the written agreement, the pharmacist can adjust the drug strength, dosing frequency, route of administration, and other aspects of drug therapy as specified in the written agreement.

Can a collaborative agreement grant a pharmacist the authority to prescribe medication or otherwise initiate drug therapy?
No. Drug therapy must be initiated by a physician.

When exercising her authority to manage drug therapy pursuant to a collaborative agreement, a pharmacist must document each intervention _____.
As soon as practicable, but no later than seventy-two (72) hours after the intervention.

If a pharmacist changes the dose, duration, or frequency of a drug pursuant to a collaborative agreement, when must the physician be notified of the change?
As soon as practicable, but no later than seventy-two (72) hours after the change.

Does a patient have the right to refuse the management of drug therapy by a pharmacist?
Yes.

How frequently must a collaborative agreement be renewed?
At least every two (2) years.

TRUE OR FALSE
A collaborative drug therapy agreement *cannot* be terminated.
False. Participation is voluntary, and a collaborative agreement can be terminated by any party at any time.

PHARMACY LAW SIMPLIFIED

PHARMACIST ADMINISTRATION OF INJECTABLES

What are the prerequisites for a pharmacist to obtain the authority to administer injectables in Pennsylvania?
- ✓ Hold an active Pennsylvania pharmacist license.
- ✓ Complete education and training in the administration of injectables within the previous two (2) years.
- ✓ Hold a current CPR certificate issued by the American Heart Association, American Red Cross, **or** a similar organization approved by the Board.

Education and training in the administration of injectables must include…
- ✓ Study material.
- ✓ A minimum of ten (10) hours of instruction and training, including a **hands-on** training session.
- ✓ Completion of an exam with a passing score.

What fee must be submitted with the application for authority to administer injectables?
$30.

When must the authority to administer injectables be renewed?
Biennially (every two (2) years) with pharmacist license renewal.

> **Note:** Must submit proof of current CPR certification for renewal.

To continue immunizing, how many credit hours of CE on the topic of immunizations must a pharmacist obtain with each license renewal?
At least two (2) out of the thirty (30)-hour biennial CE requirement must be on the topic of immunizations.

What is the fee for *renewing* the authority to administer injectables?
$30.

How much professional liability insurance must a pharmacist maintain to legally administer injectables in Pennsylvania?
Minimum coverage in the amount of $1,000,000 per occurrence or claims made.

> **Note:** Professional liability insurance may be provided by the pharmacist's employer.

Authorized pharmacists may administer injections to individuals of what age?
Individuals greater than eighteen (18) years of age; **however**, pharmacists can administer influenza immunizations using injectable or needle-free delivery methods to patients nine (9) years of age and older.

> **Note:** Greater than eighteen (18) years of age is interpreted as the day following a person's 18th birthday.

For individuals under age eighteen (18) years, _____ must be obtained prior to administering an immunization.
Parental consent.

TRUE OR FALSE
A pharmacist can delegate the task of administering injectables to a pharmacy technician.
False.

When administering injectable immunizations, what treatment guidelines should a pharmacist follow?
Treatment guidelines established by the Centers for Disease Control and Prevention (CDC), Advisory Committee on Immunization Practices (ACIP), or another competent board-approved authority.

> **Note:** For influenza immunizations given to individuals under age eighteen (18) years using injectable or needle-free delivery methods, you must follow the immunization schedule established by the CDC.

After administering an injectable, when should the patient's PCP be notified (if PCP is known)?
Within forty-eight (48) hours.

What information must be communicated to the prescriber in the notification?
- ✓ Patient's identity.
- ✓ Product administered.
- ✓ Route of administration.
- ✓ Site of administration.
- ✓ Dose administered.
- ✓ Date of administration.

If you administer immunizations pursuant to a written protocol, how frequently must the written protocol be renewed?
Every two (2) years.

What information must be communicated when notifying a physician that an injectable has been administered pursuant to a written protocol?
- ✓ Patient's identity.
- ✓ Product administered.
- ✓ Site of administration.
- ✓ Dose administered.
- ✓ Date of administration.

> **Note:** You are not required to report the ***route of administration*** for injections given pursuant to a written protocol.

If a patient has an adverse reaction to an injection, when should the patient's physician be notified?
As soon as possible, but no later than twenty-four (24) hours after learning of the event/reaction.

What information must be recorded from each injection?
- ✓ Patient's name, address, and date of birth.
- ✓ Date of administration.
- ✓ Injection site.
- ✓ Product name, dose, manufacturer, lot number, and expiration date.
- ✓ Primary care provider's name and address.
- ✓ Administering pharmacist's name or initials.
- ✓ Documentation of informed consent.
- ✓ Nature of any adverse reaction and who was notified (if applicable).
- ✓ Identification of the Vaccine Information Statement (VIS) provided.
- ✓ Date the VIS was published.
- ✓ Date and to whom the VIS was given.

How long must these records be maintained?
Two (2) years.

If a pharmacy intern completes education/training on the administration of injectables and holds a current CPR certificate, can he administer injectables under the direct, immediate and personal supervision of a pharmacist who is authorized to administer injectables?
At the time of this writing, the answer is no; however, the legislation to allow interns to administer injectables under supervision ***does*** exist. This legislation cannot be put into practice until the PA State Board of Pharmacy implements new rules and regulations. Check with the PA State Board of Pharmacy or Pennsylvania Code Title 49 Chapter 27 for updates on the relevant immunization rules and regulations.

HOSPITAL PHARMACIES

What are the space requirements for a hospital pharmacy?
The Pennsylvania Code states that there shall be adequate space provided for all pharmacy operations and storage of drugs with proper lighting, ventilation, and temperature controls.

Who is responsible for periodically checking all areas of the hospital where drugs are stored, such as drug cabinets?
The pharmacist.

Where must hospital pharmacy dispensing records be maintained?
In the pharmacy.

Where must drug administration records be maintained?
In the patient's medical record.

A record of all adverse drug reactions and drug sensitivities must be maintained in the pharmacy for how long?
For two (2) years.

Which drugs must be considered for use on a hospital's formulary?
Drugs listed on the Pennsylvania Generic Drug Formulary.

For hospital pharmacies, only drugs listed in at least one (1) of the following references may be dispensed:
- United States Pharmacopoeia.
- National Drug Formulary.
- AMA Drug Evaluation.
- Accepted Dental Remedies.
- Pennsylvania Generic Drug Formulary.
- The Physician's Desk Reference.

Note: There is an exception for experimental drugs. See below.

FDA-approved experimental drugs that are not included in any of the above-mentioned references may be used after a hospital's _____ establishes standards for use.
Pharmacy & Therapeutics Committee (P&T Committee).

Who must be on the P&T Committee?
Physicians, nurses, and pharmacists.

What is the primary function of the P&T Committee?
To assist in forming policies for all matters related to drugs in the hospital.

How frequently must the P&T Committee hold meetings?
At least quarterly.

Dangerous drugs that are prescribed for an unspecified amount of time are subject to _____.
Automatic stop procedures.

What are "dangerous drugs?"
- ✓ Controlled substances
- ✓ Sedatives
- ✓ Anticoagulants
- ✓ Antibiotics
- ✓ Oxytoxics
- ✓ Corticosteroids

TRUE OR FALSE
Emergency medication kits are stocked and approved by nurses.
False. Emergency medication kits are stocked and approved by **pharmacists**.

DRUG THERAPY PROTOCOLS

TRUE OR FALSE
In an institutional setting, a pharmacist can manage certain drug therapy on behalf of a physician pursuant to a written agreement (a drug therapy protocol).
True.

Can such an agreement be made verbally?
No. These agreements must be in writing.

Can drug therapy protocols be made in any setting?
No. Drug therapy protocols can only be made in the institutional setting. In the outpatient setting, pharmacists and physicians may form collaborative drug therapy agreements.

A practicing dermatologist forms a written agreement with a pharmacist to manage cardiovascular medications for her patients. Is this appropriate?
No, since cardiology is outside the scope of a dermatologist's practice.

You are hired as a pharmacist at a local hospital pharmacy. You are informed by a physician that you will be required to participate in a written agreement to manage drug therapy. Must you participate?
No. As with collaborative drug therapy agreements, participation in drug therapy protocols is voluntary for all parties involved. You cannot be required to participate.

To participate in a written agreement authorizing the management of drug therapy, how much professional liability insurance must you maintain?
Minimum coverage in the amount of $1,000,000 per occurrence or claims made.

> **Note:** You must maintain professional liability insurance for the duration of the written agreement.

Must you personally purchase professional liability insurance to participate in a written agreement?
No. The insurance may be purchased by your employer. The same is true for the professional liability insurance required for pharmacists who participate in collaborative agreements.

Under a written agreement, can pharmacists initiate drug therapy?
No. Drug therapy must be initiated by a physician.

When exercising her authority to manage drug therapy pursuant to a written protocol, a pharmacist must document each intervention _____.
As soon as practicable, but no later than seventy-two (72) hours after the intervention.

If a pharmacist changes the dose, duration, or frequency of a drug pursuant to a written drug therapy protocol, when must the physician be notified of the change?
As soon as practicable, but no later than seventy-two (72) hours after the change.

If a patient's drug therapy will be managed by a pharmacist pursuant to a written agreement, must the patient be notified of the pharmacist's role in advance?
Yes, and the patient has the right to refuse the management of drug therapy by a pharmacist.

Does a patient have the right to view the written agreement, or is the written agreement confidential?
The patient has the right to view the written agreement.

What is the purpose of a drug therapy protocol?
- ✓ Specifies the functions and tasks delegated to the pharmacist.
- ✓ Identifies the name of each physician and pharmacist involved in the agreement.

TRUE OR FALSE
For a drug therapy protocol to be valid, it must be signed and dated by each participating physician and pharmacist.
True.

How frequently must a drug therapy protocol be renewed?
At least every two (2) years.

TRUE OR FALSE
A drug therapy protocol *cannot* be terminated.
False. A drug therapy protocol may be terminated by any party at any time.

LONG-TERM CARE FACILITIES

Who can dispense medication in a long-term care facility?
- ✓ Pharmacists.
- ✓ Physicians (only for residents in their care).

Can residents of a long-term care facility choose the pharmacy that will dispense their medication?
Yes.

How often must a long-term care resident's medication profile be reviewed by a pharmacist?
Monthly.

In urgent situations, a facility can order up to a _____ supply of medication from a contract pharmacy different from the resident's pharmacy of choice.
Seven (7)-day.

In a long-term care facility, who is responsible for overseeing pharmaceutical services?
The Quality Assurance Committee.

How many emergency medication kits must be available in a long-term care facility?
At least one (1).

  Note: Emergency medication kits must have a breakaway lock, and the lock must be replaced after each use.

AUTOMATED MEDICATION DISPENSING SYSTEMS

What information must be recorded by an automated medication system?
The initials (or other identifier) of personnel accessing the system along with the date and time the system was accessed.

> **Note:** The resulting electronic audit trail must be readily retrievable.

Can a long-term care facility use an automated medication dispensing system if there is no onsite pharmacy?
Yes, *if* a pharmacist or pharmacist manager is under contract to dispense medications to the facility.

> **Note:** The pharmacist or pharmacist manager is responsible for supervising the system.

How often must an automated medication system be tested for accuracy?
At least every six (6) months *and* whenever changes or upgrades are made to the system.

Pharmacies that use automated medication systems must develop a written program for _____.
Quality assurance.

How long must documentation related to the quality assurance program be maintained?
Two (2) years.

If your pharmacy uses automated medication systems, there must be written plans for _____ and _____.
- ✓ Recovery from disasters.
- ✓ Preventive maintenance of the system.

Documentation of all maintenance must be kept on file in the pharmacy for how long?
Two (2) years.

PHYSICIAN ASSISTANT PRESCRIBING

TRUE OR FALSE
A physician assistant practices medicine per a written agreement with a supervising physician.
True.

When a physician assistant prescribes or dispenses a drug and the supervising physician is not physically present, how and when is the supervising physician required to be notified?
Orally or in writing within thirty-six (36) hours.

When initiating a C-II controlled substance, what amount of medication can a physician assistant prescribe?
Up to a seventy-two (72)-hour supply.

After a physician assistant initiates a C-II controlled substance, when must the supervising physician be notified?
Within twenty-four (24) hours.

If approved by the supervising physician, what amount of a C-II controlled substance can be prescribed by a physician assistant for ongoing therapy?
Up to a thirty (30)-day supply.

How does the pharmacy know whether the prescription is for initial therapy or ongoing therapy?
It must be written on the face of the prescription (initial therapy or ongoing therapy).

TRUE OR FALSE
A physician assistant that prescribes and/or dispenses controlled substances may do so using the supervising physician's DEA registration.
False. Physician assistants must obtain their own DEA number to prescribe and/or dispense controlled substances.

What information must appear on the prescription blank of a physician assistant (PA)?
- ✓ PA's name.
- ✓ PA's license number.
- ✓ Supervising physician's name.
- ✓ Supervising physician's license number.
- ✓ PA's DEA number (only required for controlled substance prescriptions)

Note: Physician assistants must sign their prescriptions with the abbreviation "PA-C" at the end.

CERTIFIED REGISTERED NURSE PRACTITIONER PRESCRIBING

Note: Certified registered nurse practitioners (CRNP) are midlevel practitioners. They are subject to limitations similar to those of physician assistants.

What information must appear on the prescription blank of a CRNP?
- ✓ CRNP's name and title.
- ✓ CRNP's certification number.
- ✓ Supervising physician's name.
- ✓ Supervising physician's license number.
- ✓ CRNP's DEA number (only required for controlled substance prescriptions)

What is the maximum amount of a C-II controlled substance that a CRNP can prescribe?
A seventy-two (72)-hour supply, regardless of whether the therapy is initial or ongoing.

When a CRNP prescribes a C-II controlled substance, when must the supervising physician be notified?
Within twenty-four (24) hours.

Are there any additional limitations on controlled substance prescribing by a CRNP?
Yes, a CRNP is also limited to prescribing a thirty (30)-day supply with no refills for C-III, IV, and V prescriptions.

CERTIFIED NURSE MID-WIFE PRESCRIBING

Note: Certified nurse mid-wives are midlevel practitioners. They are subject to limitations similar to those of a PA or CRNP.

TRUE OR FALSE
The same controlled substance prescribing limitations that apply to a CRNP also apply to a certified nurse mid-wife (CNM).
True. C-II prescriptions are limited to a 72-hour supply and C-III – IV prescriptions are limited to a 30-day supply with no refills.

What information must be included on prescription blanks used by a CNM?
- ✓ CNM's name.
- ✓ CNM's license number.
- ✓ CNM's contact information, including phone number.
- ✓ The abbreviation C.N.M. (or a similar designation).

Note: Certified nurse mid-wives must sign their prescriptions with the abbreviation "C.N.M." at the end as well.

OPTOMETRIST PRESCRIBING

Can optometrists prescribe C-II medications?
No.

What is the maximum amount of medication an optometrist can prescribe?
A six (6)-week supply.

POISONS

Poisons are categorized into two (2) schedules. What are the names of those schedules?
Schedule A and Schedule B.

What are some examples of Schedule A poisons?

- Arsenic
- Cyanide
- Fluorides
- Mercury compounds
- Phosphorus
- Thallium
- Sodium fluoroacetate
- Aconite
- Belladonna 0.004% or higher
- Cantharides
- Cocculus
- Conium
- Digitalis
- Gelsemium
- Hysocyamus
- Nux vomica 0.02% or higher
- Santonica
- Stramonium
- Strophanthus
- Veratrum

What are some examples of Schedule B poisons?

- Antimony 5% or higher
- Nitric Acid 5% or higher
- Hydrochloric Acid 10% or higher
- Hydrobromic Acid 10% or higher
- Sulfuric Acid 10% or higher
- Potassium Hydroxide 10% or higher
- Sodium Hydroxide 10% or higher
- Ammonia 5% or higher
- Chloroform 5% or higher
- Formaldehyde 1% or higher
- Nitroglycerin
- Nicotine 2% or higher

When selling a Schedule A or Schedule B poison, a label must be affixed to the poison's container. What information must appear on that label?
In red ink, the word "POISON" along with the name of the business selling it. The name of the poison must also be clearly printed on the label (ink color not specified).

To legally sell a poison, what criteria must be met?
- The buyer must be aware of the poisonous character of the substance.
- It must appear that the poison is to be used for a legitimate purpose.

What is the minimum age requirement for purchasing a poison?
Age sixteen (16) years.

For which poison schedule does the law require transactions to be recorded in a logbook?
Schedule A.

What information must be logged when selling Schedule A poisons?
- ✓ Date of sale.
- ✓ Name of the buyer.
- ✓ Address of the buyer.
- ✓ Signature of the buyer.
- ✓ Name of poison sold.
- ✓ Quantity of poison sold.
- ✓ Buyer's planned use for the poison.
- ✓ Name of the person dispensing the poison.

Must the person dispensing a poison be a registered pharmacist?
Yes.

Must Schedule A poison sales be logged if dispensed pursuant to a valid prescription?
No.

Violating any of the above provisions could lead to what type of conviction?
A misdemeanor conviction.

What is the maximum penalty for violating any of the above provisions?
$300 fine and three (3) months imprisonment.

SUMMARY OF KEY POINTS REGARDING POISONS

- ✓ Poisons are divided into two (2) categories – Schedule A and Schedule B.
- ✓ Schedule A poison sales must be recorded in a logbook, unless dispensed pursuant to a prescription.
- ✓ Only pharmacists can dispense/sell Schedule A poisons.
- ✓ The label on the container of a poison must have the word "POISON" and name of the business in *red ink*.
- ✓ The label must also clearly display the name of the poison (not required to be in red ink).
- ✓ The buyer must be at least sixteen (16) years old to purchase a poison.
- ✓ The buyer must also state a legitimate use for the poison.
- ✓ Violating a provision involving poisons could result in a $300 fine and/or three (3) months imprisonment.

RADIOPHARMACEUTICALS

The patient name must appear on the label of a radiopharmaceutical prescription, yet a patient name may not be available at the time a pharmacist receives and dispenses a radiopharmaceutical. In these cases, can the pharmacist dispense the radiopharmaceutical product without a patient name?
Yes, *if* the pharmacist obtains a patient name within seventy-two (72) hours after dispensing the radiopharmaceutical.

If a dispensed radiopharmaceutical product is not assigned to a patient and is never administered to a patient, what information should the pharmacist record on the prescription in lieu of the patient's name?
The words "not used."

ADVERTISING

You invested your life savings to open an independent pharmacy. To promote your business, your partner wants to provide local physicians with prescription blanks displaying the pharmacy's name and address. What should you tell your partner?
Pennsylvania law states that no pharmacist, pharmacy owner, or pharmacist manager can provide prescribers with prescription blanks bearing the pharmacist's name or the name or address of the pharmacy.

Is it legal to advertise the sale of controlled substances to the public?
No.

Prescription drug advertisements must be...
- ✓ Truthful.
- ✓ Reasonable.
- ✓ Informative.
- ✓ Understandable to the public.

NALOXONE

Can pharmacies in Pennsylvania dispense naloxone to individuals without a prescription?
Yes. On October 28, 2015, the Pennsylvania Physician General signed a standing order that allows pharmacies to dispense naloxone to all people permitted under Act 139.

Under Act 139, who can obtain naloxone without a prescription?
First responders (e.g. law enforcement, firefighters, EMS) *and* anyone at risk of experiencing an opioid overdose, including family, friends, or any other person who may be in a position to assist such a person.

By responding to a potential opioid overdose, are you exposing yourself to increased legal liability?
No. Act 139 provides immunity for people who respond to (or report) overdoses.

CONTROLLED SUBSTANCES
SELECT EXAMPLES

SCHEDULE I CONTROLLED SUBSTANCES
ILLICIT DRUGS

GHB*	LSD	MDMA
Heroin	Marijuana	Psilocybin

* Xyrem® is a C-III version of GHB for narcolepsy available only through the Xyrem® REMS program.

C-I BENZODIAZEPINES

Bromazepam	Flunitrazepam *	Nitrazepam
Camazepam	Haloxazolam	Nordiazepam
Clotiazepam	Ketazolam	Oxazolam
Cloxazolam	Loprazolam	Pinazepam
Delorazepam	Lormetazepam	Tetrazepam
Ethyl loflazepate	Medazepam	
Fludiazepam	Nimetazepam	

* Notoriously known to be a date rape drug, thus categorized in Pennsylvania as a Schedule I controlled substance. A brand name for this medication is Rufinol®, from which the slang name "roofies" was derived.

Note: Federally, all benzodiazepines are Schedule IV controlled substances, but In Pennsylvania several benzodiazepines have been categorized as Schedule I controlled substances. Remember, when federal law and state law conflict, the more restrictive law prevails.

SCHEDULE II CONTROLLED SUBSTANCES

C-II OPIOIDS
Alfentanil (Alfenta®)
Codeine
Diphenoxylate
Fentanyl (Duragesic®, Sublimaze®)
Hydrocodone (Lortab®, Norco®, Vicodin®, Tussionex®, Hycodan®, Hydromet®)
Hydromorphone (Dilaudid®, Exalgo®)
Methadone (Methadose®)
Morphine (Kadian®, MS Contin®, Roxanol®)
Opium (raw, extract, powdered, granulated, tincture of opium)
Oxycodone (Roxicodone®, Oxycontin®, Percocet®, Endocet®)
Oxymorphone (Opana®)
Sufentanil (Sufenta®)
Tapentadol (Nucynta®)

C-II STIMULANTS
Amphetamine/Dextroamphetamine (Adderall®)
Cocaine
Dextroamphetamine (Dexedrine®)
Lisdexamfetamine (Vyvanse®)
Methamphetamine (Desoxyn®)
Methylphenidate (Ritalin®, Concerta®, Daytrana®)
Dexmethylphenidate (Focalin®)

C-II DEPRESSANTS
Amobarbital (Amytal®)
Pentobarbital (Nembutal®)
Secobarbital (Seconal®)

C-II HALLUCINOGENIC SUBSTANCE
Nabilone (Cesamet®)

SCHEDULE III CONTROLLED SUBSTANCES

C-III OPIOIDS
Paregoric
Codeine *
Morphine *
Opium *

* In low doses when supplied as a combination drug. For instance, codeine alone is a C-II opioid (technically an opiate, since derived without chemical modification from the opium poppy); however, when supplied in limited concentration in combination with acetaminophen, it is sold as the C-III pain reliever Tylenol® #3.

C-III OPIOID PARTIAL AGONIST
Buprenorphine (Subutex®, Buprenex®, Suboxone®)

C-III MIXED OPIOID AGONIST/ANTAGONIST
Nalorphine (Lethodrone®, Nalline®)

C-III STIMULANTS
Benzphetamine (Didrex®, Regimex®)
Clortermine (Voranil®)
Phendimetrazine (Bontril®)

C-III DEPRESSANTS
Barbituric acid and derivatives
Sodium oxybate (Xyrem®)
Ketamine (Ketalar®)

THESE THREE (3) SCHEDULE II DEPRESSANTS ARE CATEGORIZED AS SCHEDULE III WHEN PART OF A COMPOUND, MIXTURE, OR SUPPOSITORY:

- ✓ Amobarbital
- ✓ Pentobarbital
- ✓ Secobarbital

C-III ANABOLIC STEROIDS
Boldenone (Equipoise®)
Methandrostenolone (Dianabol®)
Nandrolone (Durabolin®)
Oxandrolone (Oxandrin®)
Oxymetholone (Anadrol®)
Stanozolol (Winstrol®)
Testosterone (Androderm®, AndroGel®, Depo®-Testosterone, Testim®)

ALL ANABOLIC STEROIDS ARE SCHEDULE III CONTROLLED SUBSTANCES

C-III HALLUCINOGENIC SUBSTANCE
Dronabinol (Marinol®)

SCHEDULE IV CONTROLLED SUBSTANCES

C-IV DEPRESSANTS (BENZODIAZEPINES)
Alprazolam (Xanax®)
Chlordiazepoxide (Librium®)
Clobazam (Onfi®)
Clonazepam (Klonopin®)
Clorazepate (Tranxene®)
Diazepam (Valium®)
Estazolam (Prosom®)
Flurazepam (Dalmane®)
Lorazepam (Ativan®)
Midazolam (Versed®)
Oxazepam (Serax®)
Temazepam (Restoril®)
Triazolam (Halcion®)

BENZODIAZEPINE DRUG NAME STEMS

With few exceptions, benzodiazepine generic names contain the drug name stem "–azepam" or "–azolam."

C-IV DEPRESSANTS (NON-BENZODIAZEPINE)
Eszopiclone (Lunesta®)
Zaleplon (Sonata®)
Zolpidem (Ambien®)

C-IV DEPRESSANTS (SEDATIVE-HYPNOTICS AND ANXIOLYTICS)
Chloral hydrate (Somnote®)
Suvorexant (Belsomra®)

C-IV DEPRESSANTS (BARBITURATES)
Barbital (Veronal®)
Phenobarbital (Luminal®)

C-IV MUSCLE RELAXANTS
Carisoprodol (Soma®)

C-IV OPIOIDS
Tramadol (Ultram®)

C-IV MIXED OPIOID AGONIST/ANTAGONISTS
Butorphanol (Stadol®)
Pentazocine (Talwin®)

C-IV STIMULANTS
Modafinil (Provigil®)
Phentermine (Adipex-P®)
Sibutramine (Meridia®)

C-IV WEIGHT-LOSS DRUGS
Lorcaserin (Belviq®)

SCHEDULE V CONTROLLED SUBSTANCES

C-V OPIOIDS
Codeine *
Diphenoxylate with atropine *

* In low doses when supplied as a combination drug. For example, codeine alone is a C-II opioid; however, when supplied in limited quantities in combination with guaifenesin, it is sold as a C-V cough suppressant (Robitussin® AC). Likewise, diphenoxylate is typically a C-II opioid; however, when supplied in limited quantities in combination with atropine, it is sold as a C-V anti-diarrheal medication (Lomotil®).

C-V DEPRESSANTS
Lacosamide (Vimpat®)
Pregabalin (Lyrica®)

C-V STIMULANTS
Pyrovalerone

CONTROLLED SUBSTANCES CHARACTERIZED BY SCHEDULE

	Rx	OTC	ABUSE & DEPENDENCE	EXAMPLE
SCHEDULE I (C-I)			HIGH	HEROIN
SCHEDULE II (C-II)	✓		HIGH	ROXICODONE® OXYCODONE
SCHEDULE III (C-III)	✓		MODERATE	ANDROGEL® TESTOSTERONE
SCHEDULE IV (C-IV)	✓		MILD	VALIUM® DIAZEPAM
SCHEDULE V (C-V)	✓	✓	LOW	CHERATUSSIN® AC GUAIFENESIN WITH CODEINE

FEDERAL PHARMACY LAW HIGHLIGHTS

WHEN FEDERAL LAW AND STATE LAW DIFFER, FOLLOW THE LAW THAT IS MORE RESTRICTIVE.
When federal law and state law differ, we must follow the law that is more restrictive. For example, federal law imposes a 5-refill limit and 6-month expiration date on C-III and C-IV controlled substance prescriptions. Per federal law, these limits do *not* apply to C-V controlled substance prescriptions; however, Pennsylvania law *does* extend the 5-refill limit and 6-month expiration date to C-V controlled substance prescriptions. So, when practicing pharmacy in Pennsylvania, we must follow the law that is more restrictive by enforcing the 5-refill limit and 6-month expiration date for C-V controlled substance prescriptions.

THE ROLE OF GOVERNMENT AGENCIES

STATE BOARD OF PHARMACY
- Creates administrative rules to regulate the practice of pharmacy.
  - Includes regulation of traditional compounding pharmacies.
- Enforces state pharmacy laws and rules to protect the health, safety, and welfare of citizens of the state.

FOOD AND DRUG ADMINISTRATION (FDA)
- Enforces drug manufacturing laws.
- Regulates certain large-scale compounding facilities known as outsourcing facilities.
- Oversees prescription drug advertising, known as "direct-to-consumer" (DTC) advertising.

DRUG ENFORCEMENT ADMINISTRATION (DEA)
- Enforces the federal Controlled Substances Act (CSA).
- Categorizes drugs with potential for abuse, addiction and dependence into controlled substance schedules.

OCCUPATIONAL SAFETY AND HEALTH ADMINISTRATION (OSHA)
- Enforces occupational health and safety laws.
  - One focus of OSHA is to reduce the risk of employee exposure to blood borne pathogens. This is particularly relevant for locations where employees routinely work with needles, as in pharmacies with a clean room or pharmacies where immunizations are administered.

FEDERAL TRADE COMMISSION (FTC)
- Regulates the advertising of over-the-counter (OTC) drugs, medical devices, cosmetics, and food products.

PHARMACY LAW SIMPLIFIED

FEDERAL CONTROLLED SUBSTANCES ACT

The federal Controlled Substances Act (CSA) is located in Title 21 of the Code of Federal Regulations, Part 1300 through 1321 (21 CFR § 1300 – 1321). This section of the study guide highlights and summarizes key points from the CSA. Citations are provided in parenthesis.

✓ The goal of the CSA is to prevent illicit drug use and distribution while allowing for legitimate medical use.

✓ This law is also known as the "Comprehensive Drug Abuse Prevention and Control Act."

✓ The Drug Enforcement Administration (DEA) is responsible for enforcing the CSA.

Note: When reading the original text of the controlled substances act, it is important to recognize that the term "practitioner" is used to describe physicians, dentists, veterinarians, scientific investigators, **pharmacies**, hospitals, or anyone else permitted to handle controlled substances. (21 CFR § 802)

ACCEPTABLE CONTROLLED SUBSTANCE PRESCRIPTION FORMATS
(21 CFR § 1306.11 & 1306.21)
C-II: Written or Electronic. *
C-III – IV: Written, Verbal, Faxed, or Electronic.
C-V: Written, Verbal, Faxed, Electronic, or OTC. **

* Special cases for Schedule II prescriptions:
#1 EMERGENCY C-II PRESCRIPTIONS – VERBAL PRESCRIPTION ORDERS PERMITTED
- Schedule II prescription may be dispensed pursuant to verbal order only in an emergency.
- Prescription must be communicated directly from the prescriber to the pharmacist.
- Pharmacist must immediately reduce the verbal prescription to writing.
- If prescriber is unknown, pharmacist must make a reasonable effort to verify validity.
- Quantity must be limited to the amount adequate to treat the patient during the emergency period.
  - The law does not provide specific quantity limits.
- Prescriber must deliver a written hardcopy prescription to the dispensing pharmacy within 7 days.
- The hardcopy prescription should be attached to and kept on file with the verbal order.

#2 FAXED C-II PRESCRIPTIONS
- Faxed prescription may serve as the "original prescription" for these three (3) patient populations:
  1) Hospice patients.
  2) Home infusion patients.
  3) Long-term care facility residents.
- For all other patient populations, faxed C-II prescriptions may be filled, but cannot be dispensed until the patient presents the original prescription. The pharmacist must verify the original prescription against the faxed prescription prior to dispensing. The pharmacy must keep the original prescription for recordkeeping purposes.

** Limited quantities of a controlled substance may be dispensed without a prescription if state law permits.

ELECTRONIC CONTROLLED SUBSTANCE PRESCRIPTIONS (21 CFR § 1306.08)
Federal law permits e-prescribing of C-II through C-V controlled substances as long as the prescriber and pharmacy use e-prescription software that meets DEA requirements.

CONTROLLED SUBSTANCE PRESCRIPTION REFILLS
C-II: Refills are **not** permitted. (21 CFR § 1306.12)
C-III – IV: Up to 5 refills. (21 CFR § 1306.22)
C-V: No maximum.

PHARMACY LAW
SIMPLIFIED

CONTROLLED SUBSTANCE PRESCRIPTION EXPIRATION
C-II: No expiration.
C-III – IV: Expires 6 months after date written. (21 CFR § 1306.22)
C-V: No expiration.

CONTROLLED SUBSTANCE PRESCRIPTION PARTIAL FILLS
C-II: Permitted at the request of the patient or prescriber as long as the remainder is filled within 30 days. If the partial fill is for an oral emergency prescription, then the remainder must be filled within 72 hours. If the remainder is not filled within the respective time frames described above, then the remainder is void and the prescriber must be notified. * (21 CFR § 1306.13 & S. 524 (CARA of 2016))
C-III – V: Permitted with no time limit for completion; however, keep in mind that C-III and C-IV prescriptions expire 6 months after the date written.
* For long-term care or terminally ill patients, multiple partial fills for Schedule II prescriptions are permitted for up to 60 days from the date written. (21 CFR § 1306.13)

SEMANTICS OF THE 5 REFILL LIMIT FOR C-III AND C-IV PRESCRIPTIONS
Mary has a prescription for 30 tablets of Ativan® with instructions to take 1 tablet by mouth nightly as needed with 5 refills. Imagine that Mary requests just 15 tablets each time she has the prescription filled.

In scenarios like the one described above, a pharmacist may consider the following…
Schedule III & IV controlled substance prescriptions are limited to 5 refills within 6 months from the date issued. If Mary receives 15 tablets per fill, must she forfeit the prescribed quantity that remains after the 5th fill?

The answer is *no*. In this case, the first 15 tablets are considered to be a "partial fill." The next 15 tablets would represent a completion of the partial fill. This cycle would continue until the patients receives all 180 tablets prescribed, or until the prescription expires, whichever comes first.

MAIN POINT: The number of times a C-III or C-IV prescription is filled is not important. What is important?

  #1 the prescriber cannot authorize more than 5 refills.
  #2 the patient cannot receive a quantity above that which is prescribed.

TRANSFERRING CONTROLLED SUBSTANCE PRESCRIPTION ORDERS FOR REFILL
C-II: Transfers are *not* permitted.
C-III – V: May be transferred to another pharmacy on a *one-time* basis between two licensed pharmacists. Transfers are unlimited for pharmacies that share a real-time, online database. (21 CFR § 1306.25)

MAINTENANCE OF CONTROLLED SUBSTANCE PRESCRIPTION RECORDS
C-II: Must be stored separate from all other prescription records. (21 CFR § 1304.04)
C-III – V: Must be stored either separate from all other prescription records, or marked in the lower right corner with the letter "C" at least 1-inch high in red ink and stored in the same file with non-controlled substance prescription records. (21 CFR § 1304.04)

CONTROLLED SUBSTANCE STORAGE & SECURITY
Controlled substances must be stored in a locked cabinet or dispersed among non-controlled stock in such a manner as to deter theft or diversion. (21 CFR § 1301.75)

DISTRIBUTING OR RECEIVING CONTROLLED SUBSTANCE INVENTORY
C-II: Use a *DEA Form 222* to document the transaction. * (21 CFR § 1305.03)
C-III – V: Use an *invoice* to document the transaction.
* The Controlled Substance Ordering System (CSOS) is an electronic alternative to the DEA Form 222.

THE "5% RULE" FOR PHARMACIES

Pharmacies that are registered with the DEA may distribute a limited number of controlled substance dosage units to another DEA-registered pharmacy or practitioner **without registering as a distributor**. The limit is 5% of the total number of controlled substance dosage units dispensed during one (1) calendar year.

TO DISPENSE A QUANTITY OF CONTROLLED SUBSTANCE DOSAGE UNITS IN EXCESS OF 5% OF THE TOTAL QUANTITY DISPENSED DURING ONE (1) CALENDAR YEAR, A PHARMACY MUST REGISTER AS A DISTRIBUTOR.

Records of distribution and receipt must be maintained for at least two (2) years.
- ✓ Executed DEA Form 222 for C-II drugs.
- ✓ Invoices for C-III, IV, and V drugs.

DISPOSAL OF CONTROLLED SUBSTANCE INVENTORY (21 CFR 1317.05)

Controlled substance inventory that is expired or otherwise unusable should be disposed of promptly by any of these methods:
- ✓ Destroy the substance on-site (i.e. in the pharmacy/facility) in the presence of a DEA agent or other authorized person.
    - o Permission from DEA must be obtained in advance. *
    - o Two (2) employees of the DEA registrant must witness destruction. (21 CFR 1317.95)
    - o No specific method of destruction is required, but the drug must be rendered "non-retrievable."
    - o Document destruction on a DEA Form 41.
- ✓ Deliver the substance to a reverse distributor.
    - o Document transaction on a DEA Form 222.
- ✓ For returns or recalls, deliver the substance to the source from which it was obtained.
    - o Document transaction on a DEA Form 222.
- ✓ Request assistance from the Special Agent in Charge at the local DEA office.
    - o Submit DEA Form 41 to the Special Agent in Charge.
    - o Wait to receive disposal instructions.

* Practitioners (i.e. prescribers, pharmacies, and hospitals) that routinely dispose of controlled substances can obtain special authorization from the DEA to dispose of controlled substances without first obtaining permission. These practitioners must maintain disposal records and report a summary of disposal activities periodically to the DEA Special Agent in Charge.

CONTROLLED SUBSTANCE DRUG WASTAGE

According to a DEA letter to registrants that was written on September 9, 2014, destruction of controlled substance drug wastage in an institutional setting, such as that which is produced when a nurse administers only a fraction of a controlled substance from a pre-filled syringe, should be recorded in compliance with 21 CFR 1304.22(c). The destruction of controlled substance drug wastage in an institutional setting should *not* be recorded on a DEA Form 41.

OTHER KEY POINTS REGARDING CONTROLLED SUBSTANCES
- A controlled substance prescription must be issued for a legitimate medical purpose in the practitioner's usual course of professional practice. (21 CFR § 1306.04)
- The dispensing pharmacist shares a corresponding responsibility with prescriber for proper prescribing and dispensing of controlled substances. (21 CFR § 1306.04)
- Post-dating prescriptions (i.e. writing an issue date on the prescription that is later than the actual date issued) is prohibited.
- Prescribers are allowed to issue multiple C-II prescriptions to the same patient for the same medication, as long as they indicate the earliest fill date on each prescription AND the total amount prescribed does not exceed a 90-day supply. (21 CFR § 1306.12)
- It is illegal for a patient to mail/ship controlled substances out of the country.
- Federal law places no limit on the number of dosage units of a controlled substance that can be authorized by prescription at one time.
- Verbal orders/prescriptions for controlled substances must be communicated directly ***from the prescriber to the pharmacist.*** To be clear, pharmacy technicians ***cannot*** accept oral prescriptions for controlled substances, and agents of the prescriber (e.g. nurses, medical assistants, and secretaries) ***cannot*** provide telephone authorization for controlled substance prescriptions. (21 CFR 1306.21)
- An agent of the prescriber (e.g. a nurse, medical assistant, or secretary) CAN fax a controlled substance prescription to the pharmacy as long as the prescription is manually signed by the prescriber prior to faxing. (21 CFR 1306.21)

REQUIRED INFORMATION FOR CONTROLLED SUBSTANCE PRESCRIPTION ORDERS (21 CFR § 1306.05)

- ✓ Patient's Full Name & Address.
- ✓ Prescriber's Full Name & Address.
- ✓ Prescriber's DEA Number.
- ✓ Drug Name, Strength, & Dosage Form.
- ✓ Quantity Prescribed.
- ✓ Directions for Use.
- ✓ Date Issued.
- ✓ Prescriber's Signature (*not* required for verbal prescriptions).

DEA REGISTRATION

- ✓ Required for all practitioners who prescribe controlled substances and all entities involved in the production and/or distribution of controlled substances. Registrants receive a DEA number.
  - ✓ DEA registrations must be renewed once every 3 years.

OVER-THE-COUNTER CONTROLLED SUBSTANCE SALES (21 CFR § 1306.26)

Limited quantities of controlled substances may be dispensed without a prescription if state law permits.

LIMITS
- ✓ 8 ounces (240 mL) of an opium-containing liquid drug product.
- ✓ 4 ounces (120 mL) of a liquid that contains a controlled substance other than opium.
- ✓ 48 dosage units of an opium-containing solid drug product.
- ✓ 24 dosage units of a solid drug product that contains a controlled substance other than opium.

RECORDKEEPING REQUIREMENTS
- ✓ Purchaser must be at least 18 years-old.
- ✓ Purchaser must furnish ID.
- ✓ The pharmacy must record:
  - o Name & address of purchaser.
  - o Name & quantity of controlled substance sold over-the-counter.
  - o Date of sale.
  - o Name or initials of dispensing pharmacist.

Per 21 CFR § 1304.04, controlled substance records must be kept for at least 2 years.

CONTROLLED SUBSTANCE INVENTORY REQUIREMENTS (21 CFR § 1304.11)

INITIAL INVENTORY
An initial inventory must be taken when a pharmacy first opens for business.

BIENNIAL INVENTORY
Entire controlled substance inventory must be counted at least once every 2 years.

NEWLY SCHEDULED DRUG OR CHANGE IN SCHEDULE OF A DRUG
When a drug is newly scheduled as a controlled substance or the scheduling of a drug is changed, an inventory is required for the affected drug on the day that the scheduling or change in scheduling takes effect.

INVENTORY COUNTING PROCEDURES

For C-II controlled substances, an *exact count* or measure of every container is required regardless of size.
For C-III, C-IV, and C-V controlled substances...
- ✓ An *estimate* or exact count is acceptable for opened containers that hold ≤ 1,000 tablets or capsules.
- ✓ An *exact count* is required for opened containers that hold >1,000 tablets or capsules.

Note: Controlled substance *drug samples* are not exempt from inventory requirements.
Per 21 CFR § 1304.04, controlled substance records must be kept for at least 2 years.

DRUG ADDICTION TREATMENT ACT OF 2000 (DATA 2000)

- ✓ Allows prescribers to obtain a waiver so they can prescribe Schedule III, IV, and V controlled substances for the treatment of opioid addiction outside of a registered narcotic treatment facility.

- ✓ Does NOT permit the prescribing of Schedule II controlled substances (i.e. methadone) for the treatment of opioid addiction outside of a registered narcotic treatment facility.

- ✓ Prescribers who have obtained the waiver possess a second DEA number that begins with the letter X.

METHADONE DISPENSING RESTRICTIONS

Only registered narcotic treatment facilities can dispense Schedule II controlled substances (i.e. methadone) for the treatment of opioid addiction. These facilities must complete a DEA Form 363 to apply for DEA registration.

DISPENSING METHADONE FROM A PHARMACY

⇨ Dispensing methadone for the treatment of *pain* is *permitted*.
⇨ Dispensing methadone for the treatment of *addiction* is *prohibited*.

DEA FORMS

The Drug Enforcement Administration (DEA) is responsible for enforcing the federal Controlled Substances Act (CSA). The DEA's goal is to ensure that controlled substances are available for legitimate medical and research purposes, while preventing illicit use and illegal distribution. To accomplish this, the DEA strictly monitors the manufacturing, distribution, and dispensing of controlled substances. Consequently, extensive documentation is required for legitimate handling of controlled substances. To standardize recordkeeping procedures, the DEA provides preformatted forms for pharmacies and other individuals/entities that handle controlled substances. Use the chart below to memorize the titles of the most commonly used forms ("DEA Form Number") and their associated purposes.

FORM NUMBER	PURPOSE
DEA Form 41	For reporting the destruction of controlled substances.
DEA Form 104	For reporting a pharmacy closure or surrender of a pharmacy permit.
DEA Form 106	For reporting the loss or theft of controlled substances.
DEA Form 222	For ordering Schedule I & II controlled substances.
DEA Form 222a	For ordering an additional supply of DEA 222 forms.
DEA Form 224	For applying for a DEA registration number.
DEA Form 224a	For renewing DEA registration (renewal is required every 3 years).

In pharmacy, the most commonly used DEA form is the DEA Form 222. For that reason, pharmacists should be very familiar with this particular form and its use. See below for an outline of important details:
Each DEA Form 222 includes 2 carbon copies (the original, plus 2 attached copies):
1) The first page (the original) is brown.
    o Must be retained by the drug supplier.
2) The second page (the first carbon copy) is green.
    o Must be forwarded to the DEA by the drug supplier.
3) The third page (the second carbon copy) is blue.
    o Must be retained by the pharmacy.

MISTAKES CANNOT BE CORRECTED

In the event of an error, all copies of the DEA Form 222 must be voided and retained by the pharmacy.

REAL-WORLD SCENARIO

When ordering Schedule II controlled substances for your pharmacy, what must you do with the first two pages (brown and green) of the DEA Form 222?
Give them to the supplier without separating them. For the form to be valid from the supplier's perspective, the brown and green copies must be intact with the carbon paper between them. The pharmacy must retain the third page (blue copy) of the form for recordkeeping purposes.

Note: Pharmacies must keep all controlled substance records (including executed DEA forms) for at least 2 years.

ELECTRONIC ALTERNATIVE TO THE DEA FORM 222

The Controlled Substance Ordering System (CSOS) is an electronic alternative to the DEA Form 222.

PROFESSIONALS WITH PRESCRIBING AUTHORITY

There are two categories of prescribing authority: full authority and limited authority. Four types of healthcare practitioners have full prescribing authority: licensed physicians, dentists, podiatrists, and veterinarians. These practitioners can prescribe any medication **within their scope of practice**. This means veterinarians cannot prescribe medication for humans, dentists cannot prescribe medication for conditions of the eye, etc. Below, we have illustrated the four types of healthcare professionals and the respective academic degrees that confer full prescribing authority. Keep in mind, in addition to meeting the educational requirements, these practitioners must also obtain a license by passing certain board examinations and meeting other regulatory requirements.

PRACTITIONERS WITH <u>FULL</u> PRESCRIBING AUTHORITY

PHYSICIANS	PODIATRISTS
Doctor of Medicine (MD)	Doctor of Podiatric Medicine (DPM)
Doctor of Osteopathic Medicine (DO)	

DENTISTS	VETERINARIANS
Doctor of Dental Medicine (DMD)	Doctor of Veterinary Medicine (DVM)
Doctor of Dental Surgery (DDS)	

Optometrists and midlevel practitioners have limited prescribing authority. Depending on the state in which they practice, optometrists have certain restrictions and/or limitations regarding what they can prescribe, especially when it comes to controlled substances. The same is true for midlevel practitioners, such as physician assistants and nurse practitioners. Additionally, midlevel practitioners can only prescribe specific medications as outlined in a signed, written agreement with their supervising physician. A licensed physician must approve every prescription written by a midlevel practitioner.

PRACTITIONERS WITH <u>LIMITED</u> PRESCRIBING AUTHORITY

OPTOMETRISTS	MIDLEVEL PRACTITIONERS
Doctor of Optometry (OD)	Physician Assistant (PA)
	Nurse Practitioner (NP)

Note: Some states grant limited prescribing authority to additional groups of qualified healthcare professionals, such as certified nurse midwives, certified registered nurse anesthetists, chiropractors, and registered pharmacists.

PHARMACY LAW
SIMPLIFIED

DEA NUMBER VERIFICATION

Sample DEA#: MH4836726

A prescriber cannot legally issue a controlled substance prescription unless he/she possesses a valid DEA registration number. That number must appear on the face of every controlled substance prescription issued by the prescriber. You may want to verify a DEA number before dispensing a controlled substance, especially if forgery is suspected. DEA numbers are composed of 2 letters followed by 7 numbers. First, we will review the letters.

THE 1ST LETTER: Functions to identify the type of practitioner/registrant.
- A, B, or F for physicians, dentists, veterinarians, hospitals, and pharmacies.
- M for midlevel practitioners.
- P or R for manufacturers, distributors, researchers, and narcotic treatment programs.

> **Note:** Practitioners with a waiver to prescribe buprenorphine (e.g. Subutex® and Suboxone®) for the treatment of opioid addiction outside of a narcotic treatment facility have a second DEA number, which begins with the letter X.

THE 2ND LETTER: Matches the first letter of the prescriber's last name or the first letter of the business name.

Once the letters have been verified, proceed to the 4-step process for the verifying the numerical portion of a DEA number, which is outlined below.

THE 4-STEP PROCESS FOR VERIFYING THE NUMERICAL PORTION OF A DEA NUMBER:

---------STEP 1---------
Add the 1st, 3rd, and 5th digits of the DEA number.

---------STEP 2---------
Add the 2nd, 4th, and 6th digits of the DEA number and multiply the sum by 2.

> **Note:** Remember to multiply the correct set of numbers by 2. Many students mistakenly multiply the sum of the 1st, 3rd, and 5th digits by 2 and get the wrong answer.

---------STEP 3---------
Add your answers from STEP 1 and STEP 2.

---------STEP 4---------
The sum obtained in STEP 3 will be a 2-digit number. If the DEA number is legitimate, then the second digit of this 2-digit number will match the 7th and final digit (known as the "check digit") of the DEA number.

➲ TRY IT YOURSELF! ➳

Analyze the sample DEA# shown at the top of this page. You should conclude that the number is valid. Once finished, continue to the "practice problem" shown on the following page.

FEDERAL GOVERNMENT PRACTITIONER EXEMPTION [21 CFR § 1301.23]

Practitioners who are officials of the US Army, Navy, Marines, Air Force, Coast Guard, Public Health Service, or Bureau of Prisons are not required to register with the DEA to prescribe controlled substances, unless they work in private practice. In place of the DEA number, these practitioners must indicate their branch of service or the agency in which they serve and their service identification number (e.g. Army 123-45-6789).

PHARMACY LAW
SIMPLIFIED

DEA NUMBER VERIFICATION
PRACTICE PROBLEM

VERIFY THE DEA NUMBER DISPLAYED BELOW.

John Smith, MD
DEA # FS8524616

SOLUTION

THE 1ST LETTER: The registrant is a physician (MD), so the first letter must be "A, B, or F."
THE 2ND LETTER: The prescriber's last name is Smith, so the second letter must be "S."

---------STEP 1---------

Add the 1st, 3rd, and 5th digits of the DEA number.

⇨ The sum of the 1st, 3rd, and 5th numbers (8 + 2 + 6) is 16.

---------STEP 2---------

Add the 2nd, 4th, and 6th digits of the DEA number and multiply the sum by 2.

⇨ The sum of the 2nd, 4th, and 6th numbers (5 + 4 + 1) is 10, and 10 x 2 = 20.

Note: Remember to multiply the correct set of numbers by 2. Many students mistakenly multiply the sum of the 1st, 3rd, and 5th digits by 2 and get the wrong answer.

---------STEP 3---------

Add your answers from STEP 1 and STEP 2.

⇨ The sum of 16 and 20 is 36.

---------STEP 4---------

Verify that the final digit of your answer from STEP 3 matches the check digit of the DEA number.

⇨ The final digit of the answer from STEP 3 is the number 6, which matches the check digit of the DEA number.

✓

**ACCORDING TO THE ANALYSIS OUTLINED ABOVE,
THIS DEA NUMBER APPEARS TO BE LEGITIMATE.**

Note: The Drug Addiction Treatment Act of 2000 (DATA 2000) requires prescribers to include their special DEA number (which begins with the letter X) on buprenorphine prescriptions issued for the treatment of opioid addiction. For example, Dr. John Smith's special DEA number (if he had one) would look like this: XS8524616.

INSTITUTIONAL DEA NUMBERS

When acting in the usual course of employment, practitioners and residents working for an institution (e.g. hospital) may prescribe controlled substances using the institution's DEA number. Institutions must assign an internal code number to each practitioner. The practitioner must append this code to the end of the institution's DEA number when writing prescriptions for controlled substances. See below for an example.

INSTITUTION'S DEA NUMBER	PRACTITIONER'S INTERNAL CODE
⇩	⇩
AB8524616 -	1234

Each institution must keep a list of practitioners and their assigned internal codes to enable other DEA registrants, such as pharmacies, to contact the institution and verify that a particular practitioner is authorized to prescribe controlled substances.

COMBAT METHAMPHETAMINE EPIDEMIC ACT OF 2005 (CMEA)

This law imposes regulations on the over-the-counter sale of solid dosage forms (including gel caps) that contain pseudoephedrine, ephedrine, and phenylpropanolamine. These substances are precursors to either amphetamine or methamphetamine.

PRECURSOR		POTENTIAL END PRODUCT
Pseudoephedrine	⇨	Methamphetamine
Ephedrine	⇨	Methamphetamine
Phenylpropanolamine	⇨	Amphetamine

PRIOR TO PURCHASING, THE CUSTOMER MUST FURNISH PHOTO ID.

OTC PURCHASE LIMITS
- ✓ Daily Limit: 3.6 grams/day per customer
- ✓ Monthly Limit: 9 grams/month per customer

Per 21 CFR § 844(a), a maximum of 7.5 grams of the monthly 9-gram limit can be obtained by mail.

PHARMACY RECORDKEEPING REQUIREMENTS
- ✓ Product name & quantity sold.
- ✓ Name, address, & signature of purchaser.
- ✓ Date & time of sale.

Records must be maintained for at least 2 years.

LIMITS DO NOT APPLY WHEN OBTAINED BY PRESCRIPTION.

PHARMACY STORAGE REQUIREMENT
Solid dosage forms (including gel caps) that contain pseudoephedrine, ephedrine, or phenylpropanolamine must be stored behind the pharmacy counter or in a locked cabinet away from customers.

MANUFACTURER PACKAGING REQUIREMENT
Solid dosage forms (including gel caps) that contain pseudoephedrine, ephedrine, or phenylpropanolamine must be packaged in blister packs (see illustration below).

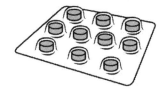

POISON PREVENTION PACKAGING ACT OF 1970 (PPPA)

- ✓ Enacted to reduce the incidence of death and serious injury caused when children access and consume medications and other dangerous household substances (e.g. household cleaning agents).

- ✓ Requires most medications to be dispensed in child-resistant packages (e.g. child safety caps on prescriptions dispensed from a pharmacy).

- ✓ Containers must be **significantly difficult** for children under 5 years-old to open, but not difficult for adults.

- ✓ Exceptions to the child-resistant packaging requirement include...
    - Nitroglycerin Sublingual Tablets
    - Steroid Dose Packs
    - Aerosols
    - Birth Control Pills
    - Female Hormone Replacement Drugs

> **NITROGLYCERIN SUBLINGUAL TABLETS ARE THE MOST NOTEWORTHY EXCEPTION TO THE CHILD-RESISTANT PACKAGING REQUIREMENT.**

If an adult has difficulty with or is unable to open a prescription bottle equipped with a child safety cap (e.g. due to arthritis), then the patient may request an easy-open cap (also referred to as a "snap cap"). The prescribing practitioner may also request an easy-open cap on behalf of the patient by making a notation on the face of the prescription.

OMNIBUS BUDGET RECONCILIATION ACT OF 1990 (OBRA '90)

- ✓ Requires pharmacists to perform prospective drug utilization reviews (DURs) and offer counseling to Medicaid patients. When performing a DUR, the pharmacist should look for things like...
    - Therapeutic duplications.
    - Drug-disease contraindications.
    - Drug-drug interactions.
    - Incorrect doses.
    - Inappropriate durations of treatment.
    - Drug-allergy interactions.
    - Clinical abuse/misuse.

- ✓ To contract with Medicaid, pharmacies must implement standards to provide counseling to Medicaid patients. The "offer to counsel" requirement does not apply in inpatient settings.

- ✓ Pharmacists must make a reasonable effort to keep patient profiles up-to-date.

- ✓ This specific law pertains only to Medicaid patients, but states have expanded it to apply to all patients.

HEALTH INSURANCE PORTABILITY & ACCOUNTABILITY ACT (HIPAA)

Protects the privacy and security of patient medical records and health information ("protected health information" or "PHI").

HIPAA PRIVACY RULE
- ✓ Limits the use and disclosure of protected health information (PHI) to the "minimum necessary."
- ✓ Provides an option for the patient to obtain a copy of their health record and request corrections.

HIPAA SECURITY RULE
- ✓ Requires various administrative, physical, and technical safeguards to ensure the confidentiality, integrity, and overall security of protected health information including electronic medical records.
- ✓ Outlines national standards for healthcare providers, insurance companies, and healthcare financial claim processing companies to protect the privacy of individual health information.

HIPAA BREACH NOTIFICATION RULE
- ✓ If protected health information has been exposed to unauthorized individuals, the affected patient(s) must be notified.

WHEN "MINIMUM NECESSARY USE AND DISCLOSURE" DOES NOT APPLY
- Disclosures to a healthcare provider for treatment.
- Disclosures to the patient upon request.
- Disclosures authorized by the patient.
- Disclosures necessary to comply with other laws.
- Disclosures to the Department of Health and Human Services (HHS) for a compliance investigation, review, or enforcement.

PRACTICAL MEASURES FOR PROTECTING PATIENT HEALTH INFORMATION
- Maintain a reasonable distance between the patient with whom you are speaking and other people in the area to prevent sensitive information from being overheard.
- Speak loudly enough for the patient to hear you, but not loud enough for bystanders to hear.
- Do not shout to a patient when discussing PHI such as medication names, medical conditions, date of birth, address, and other sensitive information.
- Never gossip about a patient and their medical information.
- Do not disclose PHI to anyone over the phone who is not legitimately entitled the information.

GENERIC SUBSTITUTION AND THE ORANGE BOOK

Prescribers often issue prescriptions for brand name drug products, but we help patients save a lot of money by dispensing generic equivalents. Another term for "generic equivalent" is "therapeutic equivalent." Compared to a brand product, the generic or therapeutic equivalent is equal in terms of strength, quality, performance, safety, intended use, dosage form, route of administration, and rate and extent of absorption... pretty much every category that matters from a medical and scientific standpoint. The only difference between a brand product and a generic equivalent is the identity of the manufacturer and the composition of inactive ingredients (e.g. fillers, binders, and color additives).

THE FEDERAL ORANGE BOOK

✓ Official Title: Approved Drug Products with Therapeutic Equivalence Evaluations

DETERMINATION OF THERAPEUTIC EQUIVALENCE

The Federal Orange Book contains a listing of "TE codes" (therapeutic equivalence codes) for generic drug products. Products with a TE code beginning with the letter A are deemed to be therapeutically equivalent to the brand name product. Pharmacists commonly refer to these products as "A-rated generics."

REAL-WORLD SCENARIO

You receive a prescription for Lipitor® over the telephone. Should you dispense brand name Lipitor® or the generic equivalent, atorvastatin?
Atorvastatin. If the prescriber (or his/her agent) expressly stated that the brand name is necessary and substitution is not permitted, then it would have been appropriate to dispense the brand name version instead.

NARROW THERAPEUTIC INDEX DRUGS

A narrow therapeutic index (NTI) drug is a medication that requires careful dose titration and patient monitoring for safe & effective use. For a drug to be considered "NTI," one of the following two conditions must apply:
- There is less than a 2-fold difference between the median lethal dose (LD50) and the median effective dose (ED50).
- There is less than a 2-fold difference between the minimum toxic concentration (MTC) and the minimum effective concentration (MEC).

Note: ED50 is the dose that produces the desired effect in 50% of the population, and LD50 is the dose that is lethal in 50% of the population.

TRUE OR FALSE

A BRAND NAME NARROW THERAPEUTIC INDEX DRUG SHOULD NOT BE SUBSTITUTED WITH A GENERIC DRUG.
It depends. The pharmacist must use professional judgement combined with regulatory knowledge to make the final determination in any generic substitution decision.

FEDERAL FOOD, DRUG & COSMETIC ACT (FD&C ACT)

The first federal law to regulate drug products was the Pure Food and Drug Act of 1906. This legislation addressed purity, but did not address safety or prohibit false claims. In 1938, the Pure Food and Drug Act was replaced by the Food, Drug, and Cosmetic Act (FD&C Act) This new legislation required drug manufacturers to provide the FDA with evidence of safety by submitting a New Drug Application (NDA); however, if action was not taken by the FDA within 60 days, the drug was automatically approved. The FD&C Act has undergone several amendments since it was first passed in 1938. In this section of the study guide, we highlight key amendments and their impact on the practice of pharmacy.

DURHAM-HUMPHREY AMENDMENT (1951)
- ✓ Drug products are separated into two categories: over-the-counter and prescription-only ("legend drugs").
- ✓ Legend drug labels must state, "Caution: Federal law prohibits dispensing without a prescription."

KEFAUVER HARRIS AMENDMENT (1962)
- ✓ Passed in reaction to "The Thalidomide Tragedy," which took place between 1957 – 1961.
- ✓ To obtain FDA approval for a drug, manufacturers must provide substantial evidence of safety and efficacy.
- ✓ Previously, New Drug Applications gained automatic approval after 60 days if the FDA did not take action. With this amendment, manufacturers must prove safety regardless of the time frame.
- ✓ In the past, manufacturers were not required to prove efficacy.

FEDERAL ANTI-TAMPERING ACT (1982)
- ✓ Passed in reaction to the "Chicago Tylenol® Murders," which took place in 1982.
- ✓ Over-the-counter (OTC) drug products must have a tamper-evident seal.

PRESCRIPTION DRUG MARKETING ACT OF 1987 (PDMA)
- ✓ Banned the selling/purchasing/trading of prescription drug samples.

The Dietary Supplement Health and Education Act of 1994 (DSHEA)
- ✓ Dietary supplements (e.g. vitamins, minerals, herbal supplements) are classified as "food" since they supplement the diet. As a result, manufacturers can market dietary supplements without FDA review.
- ✓ For drug products, a manufacturer must prove safety before entering the market, but for food products the FDA must prove lack of safety to be able to take a product off the market.

FOOD AND DRUG ADMINISTRATION MODERNIZATION ACT OF 1997 (FDAMA)
- ✓ The statement required to appear on legend drug labels per the Durham-Humphrey Amendment ("Caution: Federal law prohibits dispensing without a prescription") could be shortened to "Rx only."

ADULTERATED VS MISBRANDED

ADULTERATED	MISBRANDED
Problem(s) with the ***product***, such as the...	Problem(s) with the ***labeling***, such as...
✓ Strength of the product.	✓ False information.
✓ Quality of the product.	✓ Misleading information.
✓ Purity of the product.	✓ Insufficient information.

COMPOUNDING VS MANUFACTURING

When pharmacies cross the line into manufacturing, they expose themselves to many legal/regulatory liabilities. For instance, manufacturers must obtain a drug manufacturer permit and register with the FDA prior to commencing operation. Manufacturers are also required to comply with current good manufacturing practices (CGMP). Compounding pharmacies do not share these burdens.

THE DEFINITION OF COMPOUNDING

Compounding is the creation of personalized, patient-specific medications.

⇨ A compounded drug product **cannot be a copy** of a commercially available FDA-approved product. *
⇨ A compounded drug product cannot contain any ingredient that has been deemed unsafe or ineffective.
⇨ A product can **only** be compounded **after** receiving an individual, patient-specific prescription order **or** in anticipation of receiving a patient-specific prescription order **if** an established prescribing pattern exists.

* Possible exception in the event of a shortage.

Compounding must take place in a registered pharmacy under the supervision of a licensed pharmacist. Manufacturing must take place in a registered drug manufacturing facility.

OUTSOURCING FACILITIES

Per the Drug Quality and Security Act of 2013, certain large-scale compounding facilities must register with the FDA as **outsourcing facilities** and comply with current good manufacturing practices (CGMP).

REGULATED BY...	TRADITIONAL PHARMACIES	OUTSOURCING FACILITIES	MANUFACTURING FACILITIES
STATE BOARD OF PHARMACY	✓	✓	✓
FOOD AND DRUG ADMINISTRATION		✓	✓

PHARMACY LAW
SIMPLIFIED

MEDICAID TAMPER-RESISTANT PRESCRIPTION REQUIREMENT

Written outpatient prescriptions billed to Medicaid must be written on tamper-resistant paper to reduce the incidence of Medicaid insurance fraud. The tamper-resistant prescription paper requirement does NOT apply to prescriptions transmitted by...
- Phone.
- Fax.
- E-prescription.

For prescription paper to fulfill the tamper-resistant requirement, the paper must contain each of the following three (3) security features:
- At least one (1) feature to prevent unauthorized copying.
    - EXAMPLE: The word "VOID" or "ILLEGAL" appearing in the background when photocopied.
- At least one (1) feature to prevent erasure or modification of information written by the prescriber.
    - EXAMPLE: Checkboxes for quantities/refill authorizations or background ink that shows erasures.
- At least one (1) feature to prevent the use of counterfeit prescription forms.
    - EXAMPLE: Serial numbers or logos printed on the prescription paper.

If any of the required security features are not present on the prescription paper, the pharmacy may obtain verbal confirmation of the order from the prescribing practitioner to satisfy the tamper-resistant requirement.

LAW
PUBLIC LAW 110-28 Section 7002(b)
US Troop Readiness, Veterans' Care, Katrina Recovery, and Iraq Accountability Appropriations Act 2007

GUIDANCE DOCUMENTS
Available at <https://www.cms.gov/medicare-medicaid-coordination/fraud-prevention/fraudabuseforprofs/trp.html>

FDA RECALLS

CLASS I RECALL
Use of (or exposure to) the recalled product will cause serious adverse health effects up to and including death.

CLASS II RECALL
Use of (or exposure to) the recalled product may cause temporary or medically reversible adverse health effects.

CLASS III RECALL
Use of the recalled product is unlikely to cause adverse health effects.

REVIEW QUESTION

What is the most serious class of FDA recall?
The class I recall.

NDC NUMBERS

A National Drug Code (NDC) number is an 11-digit number composed of three (3) parts. The first part identifies who manufactured the product, the second part identifies what the product is, and the third part typically identifies the size of the package or the quantity of dosage units contained in the package. The standard format of an NDC number is as follows:

12345–1234–12

First Segment (5 digits)
The first segment of an NDC number identifies the manufacturer of the product (e.g. 00093 is the 5-digit code for TEVA and 52544 is the 5-digit code for Watson Pharmaceuticals).

Second Segment (4 digits)
The middle segment of an NDC number identifies the product made by the manufacturer (e.g. 0913 is Watson Pharmaceutical's 4-digit code for Norco® 5/325 mg).

Third Segment (2 digits)
The last segment of an NDC number usually identifies the package size of the product (e.g. the NDC number for a 100-tablet bottle of Watson Pharmaceutical's Norco® 5/325 mg is 52544-0913-01; whereas, the NDC number for a 500-tablet bottle is 52544-0913-05).

Note: In most cases, a leading zero is omitted from the NDC number displayed on the label of the manufacturer's stock bottle. For instance, the 11-digit NDC 00093-0287-01 would typically be displayed in one of the following three formats:

0093-0287-01
00093-287-01
00093-0287-1

PHARMACY LAW
SIMPLIFIED

OVER-THE-COUNTER DRUG LABELS
WHY PHARMACIES SHOULD AVOID RE-PACKAGING OTC BULK BOTTLES

Over-the-counter (OTC) drugs have strict and extensive labeling requirements that are enforced by the FDA. For this reason, it is generally not a good idea for pharmacies to re-package the contents of bulk over-the-counter drug bottles into smaller containers for resale.

OUTLINE OF INFORMATION REQUIRED TO APPEAR ON AN OTC DRUG PACKAGE LABEL (21 CFR § 201.66)

- DRUG FACTS
    - Active Ingredient(s) and strength or concentration per dosage unit.
    - Purpose(s).
- USE(S)
- WARNING(S)
- DIRECTIONS
    - Specific instructions based on age, recommended dose, frequency of dosing and maximum daily dose.
- OTHER INFORMATION
    - Storage requirements.
- INACTIVE INGREDIENTS
    - List of ingredients that do not affect therapeutic action, such as flavoring agents, colorants, and preservatives.
- CONTACT INFORMATION
    - Name, location, and phone number of the manufacturer.
- **Per 21 CFR § 211.132, a statement regarding the integrity of the tamper-evident packaging, such as "Do not use if safety seal is broken or missing."** *

---

* The FDA requires tamper-evident packaging for most OTC medications. This requirement was established after the 1982 Chicago Tylenol® Murders, where someone laced Tylenol® capsules with cyanide and returned the bottles to the shelf killing seven people.

RESTRICTED DRUG PROGRAMS

As we know, medications have potential benefits (the intended therapeutic effect) and risks (side effects). Drugs that cause more harm than good typically do not reach the market, or, if they have already entered the market, are withdrawn once the harm is recognized (e.g. Vioxx®). Some medications are capable of causing great harm and yet provide tremendous benefits for certain patients. This is where restricted drug programs come into play. Pursuant to the FDA Amendments Act of 2007, the FDA can require manufacturers to comply with programs that help manage the risks associated with the use of certain drugs. These programs are also referred to as "Risk Evaluation and Mitigation Strategies" (REMS). Over 100 drugs are associated with a REMS program. The most well-known REMS programs are iPLEDGE™, THALOMID REMS™, T.I.P.S., and Clozaril® National Registry. In this section of the study guide, we review the basic elements of each of these four programs.

iPLEDGE™
Isotretinoin is effective in the treatment of severe acne; however, the use of isotretinoin during pregnancy is associated with severe birth defects. Among other requirements, iPLEDGE™ primarily mitigates this risk by...

1) Ensuring that patients who begin isotretinoin therapy are not pregnant.
2) Preventing pregnancy in patients who receive isotretinoin.

OTHER IMPORTANT POINTS:
- ✓ Isotretinoin prescriptions are limited to a 30-day supply.
- ✓ Isotretinoin brand name formulations include Absorbica®, Accutane®, Amnesteem®, Claravis®, Myorisan®, Sotret®, and Zenatane®.

THALOMID REMS™ (formerly known as S.T.E.P.S.®)
Thalomid® (thalidomide) is effective in the treatment of multiple myeloma and erythema nodosum leprosum; however, the use of thalidomide during pregnancy is associated with severe birth defects (e.g. "The Thalidomide Tragedy"). Among other requirements, THALOMID REMS™ primarily mitigates this risk by...

1) Ensuring that patients who begin thalidomide therapy are not pregnant.
2) Preventing pregnancy in patients who receive thalidomide.

OTHER IMPORTANT POINTS:
- ✓ Thalidomide prescriptions are limited to a 28-day supply with no refills or telephone prescriptions.
- ✓ The THALOMID REMS™ program was previously known as S.T.E.P.S.® (System for Thalidomide Education and Prescribing Safety).

T.I.P.S.
T.I.P.S. stands for "Tikosyn® In Pharmacy System." Tikosyn® (dofetilide) is used to induce and maintain normal cardiac sinus rhythm in highly symptomatic patients with atrial fibrillation or atrial flutter; however, the use of dofetilide is associated with potentially fatal ventricular arrhythmias, especially in patients who are starting or re-starting the drug. T.I.P.S. mitigates this risk by...

1) Communicating the risk of cardiac arrhythmias associated with Tikosyn® (dofetilide).
2) Requiring patients who receive Tikosyn® (dofetilide) to be admitted to a facility for medical monitoring for at least three (3) days when starting or re-starting therapy.

Clozaril® National Registry

Clozaril® (clozapine) is effective in the treatment of various psychiatric disorders (e.g. schizophrenia, bipolar disorder); however, the use of clozapine is associated with the potentially fatal agranulocytosis (suppression of white blood cell production). Clozaril® National Registry mitigates this risk by...

1) Requiring WBC count to be recorded in the Clozaril® National Registry **weekly for the first six (6) months** of therapy and then periodically thereafter.
2) Limiting the amount of the drug pharmacies can dispense to a quantity sufficient only to treat the patient until their next scheduled lab work (e.g. a 7-day supply every week for the first six (6) months).

Note: Sometimes this REMS program is referred to as the "No Blood, No Drug Program."

EACH REMS PROGRAM IS UNIQUE

Some REMS programs are so simple that you might not even realize they exist. A great example is Dulera® (mometasone/formoterol), for which the REMS program only imposes one (1) requirement – the manufacturer must communicate to healthcare providers the increased risk of asthma-related death associated with the use of long-acting beta agonists (such as formoterol found in Dulera®). On the other end of the spectrum, we see programs like the ones discussed in this section (iPLEDGE™, Thalomid REMS™, T.I.P.S., and Clozaril® National Registry) that impose tougher rules and require participation by multiple parties (e.g. the doctor, the patient, and/or the pharmacy). Each REMS program is unique.

OTHER IMPORTANT POINTS REGARDING REMS PROGRAMS

✓ Manufacturers may implement a REMS program for a drug in the absence of an FDA requirement to do so.

✓ The consequence for a manufacturer that fails to comply with a REMS program is a fine of at least $250,000 per incident.

LONG-TERM CARE FACILITY PHARMACY SERVICES
42 CFR § 483.60

Long-term care facilities must provide (or obtain from a provider pharmacy) routine and emergency drugs and biologicals for residents.

All drugs must be stored in locked, temperature-controlled compartments. Only authorized personnel can have access to the keys.

Schedule II controlled substances and other drugs of abuse must be stored in separately locked, permanently affixed compartments, unless the facility stores a small quantity of controlled substances in single unit package drug distribution systems and missing doses can be detected readily.

Long-term care facilities must employ a pharmacist (or obtain the services of a pharmacist from a provider pharmacy) for consultation, recordkeeping, and to provide monthly drug regimen reviews for each resident.

A PHARMACIST MUST PROVIDE MONTHLY DRUG REGIMEN REVIEWS FOR EACH RESIDENT OF A LONG-TERM CARE FACILITY.

The pharmacist must report any irregularities to the physician and the facility's director of nursing, and these reports *must be acted upon* (at minimum, the pharmacist's recommendations must be acknowledged).

THE END

Copyright © 2017 by David A Heckman
All rights reserved. This content is protected by copyright. The content of this book cannot be reproduced in any form, including mechanical or electronic reproduction, without the express written permission of the author.

ADDITIONAL STUDY SOURCES
RECOMMENDED BY DAVID A HECKMAN, PHARMD

Pennsylvania Pharmacy Laws, Rules & Regulations
Pennsylvania Pharmacy Act #699
Pennsylvania Controlled Substance, Drug, Device and Cosmetic Act #64
Pennsylvania Code Title 49 Chapter 27
Pennsylvania Code Title 49 Chapter 18
Pennsylvania Code Title 28 Chapter 113
Pennsylvania Code Title 28 § 211.9
Pennsylvania Code Title 28 Chapter 25
Pennsylvania Generic Equivalent Drug Law #259

Pennsylvania State Board of Pharmacy Website
http://www.dos.pa.gov/pharm

Pennsylvania Pharmacists Association Website
http://www.papharmacists.com/page/PennsylvaniaLaws

------- *Thank You!* -------

Thank you for trusting me to help you prepare for the Pennsylvania MPJE®. I understand the responsibility and I do not take it lightly. Please consider leaving a thoughtful review online. When you provide rich feedback, it helps me figure out what works and what doesn't. Best wishes on the exam!

Sincerely,
David A Heckman, PharmD

NOTES

NOTES

NOTES

NOTES

NOTES

Made in the USA
Columbia, SC
21 July 2021